South East England
Edited by Annabel Cook

 Young Writers

First published in Great Britain in 2004 by:
Young Writers
Remus House
Coltsfoot Drive
Peterborough
PE2 9JX
Telephone: 01733 890066
Website: www.youngwriters.co.uk

All Rights Reserved

© Copyright Contributors 2004

SB ISBN 1 84460 532 9

Foreword

Young Writers was established in 1991 and has been passionately devoted to the promotion of reading and writing in children and young adults ever since. The quest continues today. Young Writers remains as committed to engendering the fostering of burgeoning poetic and literary talent as ever.

This year's Young Writers competition has proven as vibrant and dynamic as ever and we are delighted to present a showcase of the best poetry from across the UK. Each poem has been carefully selected from a wealth of *Once Upon A Rhyme* entries before ultimately being published in this, our twelfth primary school poetry series.

Once again, we have been supremely impressed by the overall high quality of the entries we have received. The imagination, energy and creativity which has gone into each young writer's entry made choosing the best poems a challenging and often difficult but ultimately hugely rewarding task - the general high standard of the work submitted amply vindicating this opportunity to bring their poetry to a larger appreciative audience.

We sincerely hope you are pleased with our final selection and that you will enjoy *Once Upon A Rhyme South East England* for many years to come.

Contents

Amy Johnson Primary School, Wallington
Joseph Forrest (9)	1
Chloe Lee (9)	1
Joe Cherry (10)	2

Beacon Hill Primary School, Hindhead
Luke Woodger (8)	3
Jamie Renninson (8)	3
Lee Reilly (8)	4
Kathryn Pearcey (9)	4
Holly Parsons (9)	5
Tom Parkes (9)	6
Jessica Hawkins (8)	6
Jack Moseley (8)	7
Emily Chaplin (9)	7
Samuel Meadowcroft (9)	8
Andrew Bingle (8)	8
Jasmin Jarman (8)	9
Mackenzie Davis (8)	9
Amy Lamont (9)	10
Kelly McMahon (9)	10
Amy Jackson (8)	11
Sam De St Croix (8)	11
Richard Cowdery (9)	12
Jason Ayling (9)	12

Beaufort Primary School, Woking
Natalie Whiten (9)	13
Ross Green (9)	13
Rosie Cranie-Higgs (10)	14
Katie Franklyn (10)	15
Linzi Davidson (10)	15
Carly Baker (10)	16
James Hopper (11)	16
Amanda Lyons (11)	17
Rebecca Hare (9)	17
Nicholas Savage (10)	18
Hannah Doe (9)	18

Lucy Hockin (9)	19
Paul Dawson (9)	19
Laura Henry (9)	20
Max Rodgers (11)	20
Charlotte Miles (10)	21
Lucy Colleer (9)	21
Jennifer Cross (10)	22
Adam Youlton (9)	22
Indeera Shankla (8)	23
Samuel Exworth (10)	24
Natalie Tunnell (8)	24
Mitchell Rogers (10)	25
Zoe Wright (10)	25
Christopher James (10)	26
Jade Mitchell (10)	26
Nathanael Osborne (10)	27
Jemma Percy (10)	28
Lewis Jones (11)	28
Emily Hopper (10)	29
Zoe Richardson (10)	30
Stephanie Withers (9)	30
Rebecca McVeigh (11)	30
Chloe Mackay (11)	31
Jade Barclay (11)	32
James Hart (10)	32
Chloe Webb (10)	33
Steven Shaw (8)	33
Joanne Burton (10)	34
Luke Reed (10)	34
Katie Thorne (11)	35
Victoria Hubbard (10)	35
Ryan Johnson (10)	36
Amy Horner (10)	36
Alexander Edwards (10)	37
Ella Vickers (10)	38
Robert Whiten (10)	38
Rebecca Lee (8)	39
Jasmin Pilott (10)	39
Liam Varndell (8)	39
Adam Tolfrey (10)	40
Stephanie Tunnell (11)	40
Charlotte Hewett (11)	41

Hannah-Louise Bryan (10) — 41
Carla Fox (10) — 42
Kellie Murray (11) — 42
Chelsea Reilly (10) — 43
Adam Dyson (11) — 43
Rachel Bell (10) — 44
Elliott Reed (10) — 44
Hadiyah Khan (11) — 45
Andrew Cruttenden (10) — 45
Mohmina Atique (10) — 46

Grand Avenue Primary School, Surbiton
Amy Akerman (9) — 46
Joel Bamber (10) — 47
Samuel Hopkins (10) — 47
Rio Edwin (10) — 48
Ji Weon Park (9) — 48
Gaayathiri Luhinthiran (9) — 49
Jackson Tyler (10) — 49
Alexander Hazzard (9) — 50
Alice Brace (10) — 50
Joshua Nicholls (10) — 50
Katie Legg (10) — 51
Kiran Gurmail (10) — 51
James Taylor (10) — 52
Louis Hebbs (10) — 52
Kajaniy Kannapiran (10) — 53
Maya Randhawa (9) — 53

Lodge School, Purley
John Caklais (7) — 54
Preten Patel (8) — 54
Kirsty Downing (8) — 55
Wei-Zheng Tan (7) — 55
Anna Caklais (9) — 56
Vishala Nadesan (8) — 56
Michael Burgoyne (9) — 57
Michael Cross (8) — 57
Dominic Bishop (9) — 57
Yasmine Heinel (9) — 58
Bilal Shariff (8) — 58

Lewis Phenix (10)	59
Bonnie Streeter (9)	59
Kian Bagheri (10)	60
Joshua Green (9)	60
Kane Rodney (9)	61
Alexander Viveash (10)	61
James Weber (10)	62
Sachin Duggal (8)	62
Andrew Ovenden (9)	63
David Omonya (10)	63

St Dunstan's CE Primary School, Cheam

Johanna Baird (8)	63
Evie Hunter Bell (9)	64
Jacob Watt (8)	64
Matthew Blackman (9)	65
Natasha Vassell (9)	65
Lydia Blagden (8)	66
Verity Patmore (8)	66
Alexander Woolford (8)	67
Grace Hunter (9)	67
Peter Buckley (10)	68
Thomas Jeavons (9)	69
Joshua Higgs (8)	69
Sian Kelly (9)	70
Phoebe Dynan-Lewis (7)	70
Tessa Caussyram (8)	70
Emily Reynolds (8)	71
Edward Blythe (7)	71
Stewart Reed (8)	71
Sophie Tonge (7)	72
Serena Shirley (7)	72
Victoria Goodridge (8)	73
Jaime-Leane Lloves (7)	73
Samuel Griffiths (8)	74
Samuel Nicholson (7)	74
Jake Worne (7)	74
Martha Hamilton (7)	75
Megan Baker (7)	75
Lucy Alder (7)	75
Alexander Tresadern (7)	76

Kieran O'Toole (7)	76
Luke Aziz (8)	77
Olivia Taylor (8)	77
Ryan Ford (8)	78
Aaron Wade (8)	78
Joshua Dawson (8)	79
Alice Bailey (7)	79
Harriet Skinner (8)	80
Alister Smith (8)	80
Jade Holyoake (7)	80
James Buxton (8)	81
Amelia Ford (7)	81
Poppy Milton-Tomkins (7)	81
Jake Heasman (9)	82
Nicholas Suchy (9)	82
Kolujo Abraham (9)	82
Sarah Dalley (10)	83
Laura Cotzias (10)	83
Lillie Garcia-Santos (7)	83
Nicholas Thomson (8)	84
Jeanie Gelling (8)	84
Alice Graves (9)	85
Aimée Nott (9)	85
Georgina Bailey (9)	86
William Tsang (8)	86
Roseanne Minnette (9)	87
Kirsty Macphie (10)	87
Joseph Murphy (9)	87
Katherine O'Reilly (9)	88
Samuel Higgs (8)	88
Brooklyn Gardner (10)	88
Ethan Hall (9)	89
Francesca Mongiovi (9)	89
Koyejo Abraham (9)	89
Kristian Childs (9)	90
Robert Reed (9)	90
Jessica Doyle (10)	90
Joshua Saliba-Graves (8)	91
Michael Buckley (9)	91
Abigail Saliba-Graves (10)	92
Georgia Rivers (10)	92
Yohannah Caussyram (9)	93

Alex Douglas (9)	93
Alida Wotherspoon (10)	94
Joseph Ahn (10)	94
Michael Crozier (8)	95
Priya McQuaid (11)	95
Savannah Worne (9)	96
Alexander Blagden (8)	96
Supanika Richmond (9)	97
Amy Swansbury (10)	97
Omar Rana (9)	97
Samuel Berry (9)	98
Benjamin Cummings-Montero (9)	98
Katy Pitcher (10)	99
Charlotte Reynolds (9)	99
Joshua Collyer (11)	100
Jaya McQuaid (8)	101
Euan McGraw (8)	101

St Dunstan's RC Primary School, Woking

Katy Munson (7)	101
Rosaleen Newell (8)	102
Shannon Southey (7)	102
Daniel Cranstone (7)	102
Georgia Taylor (7)	103
James Kear (7)	103
Olivia Ash (7)	103
Megan Turner (9)	104
Niamh Pinfield (7)	104
Natasha Dean (10)	105
Conor Edwards (7)	105
Jessica O'Callaghan (10)	106
Nathan Ghouri (7)	106
Lily Rose Smith (9)	107
Lucy Fidge (10)	108
Sophie Federico (7)	108
Charlotte Heffernan (10)	109
Helen Fenning (7)	109
Daniela Frangiamore (9)	110
Felix Reilly (8)	110
Elizabeth Fitzgerald (9)	111
Zara Mizen (8)	111

Nicholas Blackett (10)	112
Megan Hewson (7)	112
Dominique Black (11)	113
Siobhan Straver (8)	113
Matthew Kear (10)	114
Robert Derienzo (7)	114
Tom McPhee (9)	115
Vince Russo (10)	115
Hannah Spruzs (10)	116
Anna Valentino (10)	117
Amy Hull (10)	118
Luke Middleton (8)	118
David Pinfield (10)	119
Francesca Brown (10)	119
Emily Woods (8)	120
Philip Moloney (10)	120
Antonio Procida (9)	121
Lucia Caruso (9)	121
Eleanor Knecht (7)	122
Zara John (11)	122
Lucinda Piazza (7)	123
Nadia Procida (8)	123
William Grigsby (8)	124
Daniel Mulvihill (7)	124
Connor Moore (7)	125
Daniella Flint (11)	125
Jack O'Callaghan (8)	126
Cameron Grennan (8)	126
Oliver Jordan (10)	127
Cliona Moore (11)	127
Benhilda Mombo (10)	128
Carmina Gonzalez Gomez (11)	128
Roisin Straver (11)	129
Georgina Watkins (10)	130
Paul Raleigh (11)	130
Edward Wilson (10)	131
Olivia Frayne (11)	132
Christopher Ingram (10)	133
Gianluca Suppa (7)	133
Jed Tune (10)	134
Rosanna Suppa (9)	134
Andrea Avellano (11)	135

Jason Trillo (10)	135
Sarah Spears (11)	136
Ryan Hannaford (11)	136
Charlotte Harding (10)	137
Ashley Smith (10)	137
Rosemary Kelley (10)	138
Michaela Moore (10)	138
Jennifer Stedman (11)	139
Mary Rogers (11)	139

St Mary's CE Junior School, Oxted

Charlotte Penn (7)	140
Nathan Howells (9)	140
Helen Shaw (10)	141
Emma Soden (8)	141
Naomi Harris (9)	142
Jacob Willis (9)	142
Tom Munns (8)	143
Natasha Phillips (9)	143
Portia Baker (10)	143
Charlotte Dunn (8)	144
Luke Thompson (7)	144
Emma De Lange (7)	144
Terri Perks (9)	145
Sam Bowles (10)	145
Naomi Macphail (9)	145
Joshua Milne (8)	146
Sarah Cannon (7)	146
Matthew Bristow (9)	147
Annalisa Haywood (10)	147
Kate Pugh (8)	148
Emmie Claringbull (7)	148
Alessia Tomei (9)	148
Jordan Philip (10)	149
Rosie Tarrant (10)	149
James Fish (9)	149
Jacob Leach (9)	150
Anna-Leigh Casey (9)	150
Matthew Williams (8)	151
Holly Charlett (9)	151
Catherine Conquest (10)	152

Molly Borer (10)	152
Stephen Dunnell (10)	152
Megan McGeown (8)	153
Faith Willsher (9)	153
Danielle Herpe (10)	154
David Swift (10)	154
Genevieve Cox (7)	155
William Houghton (9)	155
George Jensen (9)	156
Alice Brock (8)	156
William Greenland (9)	157
Laura Dennison (8)	157
Thomas Saunders (9)	158
Jack Poole (8)	158
Meghan Sharp (9)	159
Georgina Bashford (9)	159
Alice Dickerson (9)	160
Dominic Nolan (9)	160
Emily Murphy (9)	161
Simon Barker (9)	161
Lauren Franklin (8)	162
Kenna Courtman (8)	162
Eleanor Fox (8)	163
Sarah Barratt (9)	163
Nicholas Burns (9)	164
Bronwen Craft (8)	164
Emma Moss (8)	164
Hannah Turner (8)	165

TASIS - The American School In England, Thorpe

Nicole Norman (10)	165
Olivia Krutz (11)	166
Jaimee Gundry (9)	167
Megan Yeigh (9)	168
Dylan Bole (10)	169
Anneliese Rinaldi (9)	170
Kyle Andersen (9)	171
Maggie Seymour (10)	172
Kathryn Meyer (11)	172
Timmy Davison (9)	173

Martin Sartorius (11)	173
Dominique Saayman (10)	174
Lauryn Dichting (10)	174
Sarah Lawhon (10)	175
Thurston Smalley (11)	176
Alexander Larsson (10)	176
Griffin Leeds (11)	177
Mary Buswell (11)	177
Sofia Leiva (10)	178
Emily Goode (11)	178
Matthew Buswell (9)	179
Alex Valvano (10)	180
Matthew Bayern (9)	181

Whyteleafe Primary School, Whyteleafe

Olivia Kenning (8)	181
Jessica Day (10)	182
Sarah Hugill (10)	183
Tabby Campbell (10)	184
Georgia Harbour (10)	184
Declan Bellingham (9)	185
Spencer Hall (8)	185
David Hopkins (9)	186
Amy Pocock (9)	186
Sophie Brown (10)	187
Tom Simpson (10)	188
Adam Foster (10)	189
Matthew Urquhart (10)	190
Jacob Boitel-Gill (10)	191
Sophie Read (8)	191
Georgina Barnard (11)	192
Victoria Bradford (9)	192
Rebecca Burr (10)	193
Amy Knott (9)	193
Amber Cunningham (9)	194
Peter Bowdery (9)	195
Sophie Knox (9)	196
Joanna Slevin (8)	196
Katie Sheldon (10)	197
Jasmine C Butler (9)	197

Michael Sims (11)	198
Lorna Dawe (10)	198
Eleanor Williams (10)	199
James Daly (10)	200

The Poems

The Evil Night Phantom

Evil grin increases darkness,
Violating sweet dreams
Isolated by his own power,
Lonely in the shadows.

Nightmare spread through the world,
Into his body you would see no heart,
Ghostly, ghastly, gruesome face,
Hungry for souls,
Terrifying.

Petrifying all that see him,
Hurricanes destroy the universe at dark,
Aeroplanes crash and burn because of night,
Nasty, cruel kidnapping kids,
The Grim Reaper can't take souls because of night,
Oncoming darkness freezes all that gets in the way,
Master of the shadows, master of darkness is night.

Joseph Forrest (9)
Amy Johnson Primary School, Wallington

Underwater

Underwater I can see,
An angelfish swimming round me.
The dolphins are swimming low,
The blue whale is wearing a bow.
The jellyfish are going home,
Now everyone is starting to moan.
The horrible shark is chasing me,
Now he is crying because of me.
The stingray is being nasty,
Now the turtle is being crafty.
The crab is trying to pinch me,
Now it's time for a party,
Bye-bye for now, cheerio.

Chloe Lee (9)
Amy Johnson Primary School, Wallington

My Limericks

There once was a boy called Luke
Who always used to puke
He puked in a hat
He puked on his cat
And even puked on the duke.

There once was a boy called Kayne
Who one day met David Blaine
He learned to do tricks
To levitate sticks
And after he met Bruce Wayne.

One day a boy called Joe
Was trying to learn how to sew
He tied a knot here
On top of Dad's beer
And then it started to flow.

One day a girl called Jade
Had a glass-built spade
It smashed in the sand
She had the wrong brand
She really needed first aid.

There once was a girl called Sue
Who used to live in a shoe
It really stunk
Just like a skunk
And now she lives in Peru.

There once was a boy called Mark
Who decided to build an ark
He had some faith
That it was safe
But suddenly he was eaten by a shark.

Joe Cherry (10)
Amy Johnson Primary School, Wallington

Walking Along Beacon Hill Road

I feel the lovely cool wind whistling past me,
I feel like I am sitting in front of a fan,
I am on Beacon Hill Road.

I am staring at a large rabbit's hole,
It is dark and gloomy,
It is a very long one,
I have never been so excited in my life.

I smell a large puddle of oil but where is it coming from?
I will carry on walking, I might see where it is coming from.

I am at the quite big garden, it is lovely,
Wait, there is a rabbit, it is coming towards me,
It is beautiful.

Luke Woodger (8)
Beacon Hill Primary School, Hindhead

In My Day

I am trudging along the narrow alley,
I see a garage,
I see in the garage people, they are fixing cars.

I hear a car going by, it is
Zooming.
The car looks red and shiny.

I see trees blowing,
They look like snakes,
The leaves are falling from the trees.

I feel very hungry because
I smell food,
Very nice food.

Jamie Renninson (8)
Beacon Hill Primary School, Hindhead

Big Baboons And Flying Frogs

In my teacher's cupboard are . . .
Sweets, sometimes we get six,
Pens and pencils,
Canes that can catch you.

In my teacher's cupboard is . . .
Cake for Connor and the cat next door,
Pretty patterns you picture in your head,
Badminton bats and a badminton net.

In my teacher's cupboard are . . .
Big baboons bouncing below,
Flying frog flew through the fog,
Rapid rugs rumbling.

The cupboard is hidden away,
In the darkness in the corner,
I would throw it away,
Because it's full of homework.

Lee Reilly (8)
Beacon Hill Primary School, Hindhead

A Garden Day

I can feel soft grass under my feet,
Wet, sort of, and a bit of wet soil,
On the ground of Grover's garden,

I can see leaves on the grounds that are brown,
Some of them are green ones up high in the tree,
There are yellow ones too on the ground,

I can see bare trees with a few leaves on them,
Gently through the gliding wind,
Birds come and sit on the swaying tree,

I can see a small bush sitting next to a tree,
A bird came and sat on the tree,
The bird was tweeting as well.

Kathryn Pearcey (9)
Beacon Hill Primary School, Hindhead

In My Teacher's Cupboard . . .

In my teacher's cupboard there are . . .
Moving books that move elegantly across the classroom
And land where they want,
A work printer that prints work and homework;
It knows what to do without you pressing anything,
Circling sheets that circle your subject.

In my teacher's cupboard there is . . .
A silence whistle which glues children's mouths together
So they won't talk,
Mini cameras to put around the classroom to catch the
Giggling girls whenever you can't see them,
Backwards glasses that spot bouncing boys behind you.

In my teacher's cupboard there are . . .
Put up pictures that help you so you never draw wrong,
French words so you can learn French ten times as quick,
Sheets of answers that are easy to read from a metre away.

In my teacher's cupboard there is . . .
A pocket dictionary, so if the teacher spells something wrong
It automatically changes without children seeing,
Spelling and reading books that automatically come when you need them,
Pencil cases that have pens at the top when you need them.

Holly Parsons (9)
Beacon Hill Primary School, Hindhead

Under My Secret Trapdoor

Under my secret trapdoor there is,
The scream of my sister,
The shout of my mum,
The clatter of my dad climbing up the ladder,
A little bounce of my basketball on the floor.

Under my secret trapdoor there is,
The bump, bump, bump of me going upstairs to bed,
A song off my CD player, which I left on,
The swish, swish, swishes of the swaying branches outside.

Under my secret trapdoor there is,
The strangled squeal of a mouse,
The dirty dog running round the garden,
My cat purring on my knee.

It is in the shape of a monster and the hinges are his finger joints,
There are two tall trees either side of him,
There are stars around him too.

I will sail away on my trapdoor,
Sail the seven seas until I am shipwrecked and float onto a desert island,
Where I would hopefully find food and water to the end of my days.

Tom Parkes (9)
Beacon Hill Primary School, Hindhead

The Squirrel

I can see a squirrel climbing up a bushy tree
Hopping from tree to tree
He is moving very fast
He finally gets to his squirrel home
He looks out of his house
He looks very scared of me although I do not blame him
He goes back into his home.

Jessica Hawkins (8)
Beacon Hill Primary School, Hindhead

I Can Hear . . .

I can hear cars rumbling the ground
As if there is a volcano erupting in the east
The cars are melting the snow

There is a big wooden tree hanging over me
The tree is shaped like a monster
It is hanging over me like it is solid rock

I see a big dustbin truck
It is roaring down the road
As though it is about to gobble someone up

I see a big lorry parked on a line
It is just sitting quietly
Suddenly a big vrooming sound comes out

I see a big prickly bush
It is standing there motionless
It has spikes as sharp as a hedgehog.

Jack Moseley (8)
Beacon Hill Primary School, Hindhead

Darker Than Day

Stripy green and brown snakes,
Sliding over the tree,
The tree is struggling to survive the grasp of the killer vine.

Two holes darker than day,
A smell of damp leaves,
Where is the furry creature that owns this beautiful hole?

Green prickling plants surrounding me,
They're going to kill,
Oh, they're only holly bushes.

A stump of an old tree,
The bark is rotten,
A very good stool.

Emily Chaplin (9)
Beacon Hill Primary School, Hindhead

In My Magic Rucksack

In my magic rucksack is . . .
A Game Boy that glows in the glittering dark,
A dog that digs in the daylight,
A goldfish with arms and legs.

In my magic rucksack is . . .
A bouncy ball boringly moving across the blue bat,
A soldier that slides through the safari,
A broken bracelet that bounces into the bin.

In my magic rucksack is . . .
A multicoloured moon and a blue hamster,
An elephant in the freezing cold Antarctic,
A polar bear in India.

In my magic rucksack is . . .
A bouncy-looking bat that bites balls,
A cheating cheetah that cheats in chess,
A smiley salmon that eats people.

My rucksack is made from leaves and paper,
Its lid is made from metal.
I will go to lots of different countries in my rucksack,
I will go to South Africa, Russia and Brazil.

Samuel Meadowcroft (9)
Beacon Hill Primary School, Hindhead

I Can . . .

I can see a man reading the important newspaper,
He is striding along the quiet road,
I can hear loads of cars zooming past me
And I see a motorbike,
That is very fancy,
I can smell a load of petrol and it
Is blocking my nose up,
I can see a lot of busy shops and
I see a lot of sweetie shops that
Are very nice.

Andrew Bingle (8)
Beacon Hill Primary School, Hindhead

Birds In The Snow

It is snowing; I'm going through the park gates.
The birds in the tree are talking to each other.
They are asking each other why did the snow come out today?
Tweeting puzzled.
The birds are settling on a fir tree to keep warm,
Some of them are falling asleep.
One bird is flying round my head, it is seeing what I'm doing,
It is a cute nosy robin.
They are going back to their homes to sleep
For the night.
You can see the birds flying back home gently
Settling in their nests.
That bird has just seen a few worms,
It has dived to catch them.

Jasmin Jarman (8)
Beacon Hill Primary School, Hindhead

My Imaginations

I will put in the box . . .
A microwave that is a magic meal maker
A pig that is a punk that pictures your pastime
A snake that slithers and slinks under the Scania

I will put in the box . . .
Flies that flip to the throbbing floor
A camera that clicks all clockerdy day
A pencil case that's a proper pen printer holder

I will put in the box . . .
A leopard is a large lion like
A television is antagonising TV that tiptoes through your head
A lizard that licks and loves your lungs.

Mackenzie Davis (8)
Beacon Hill Primary School, Hindhead

A Little Pink Flower

A little pink flower has just popped its head up from the wet and soggy ground,
It feels the warmth of the sun on its beautiful pink petals,
The flower will produce oxygen as its daily job.

I can see bushes of all sizes and colours,
Trees that are tall and bare in the cold wind,
I feel frozen to the bone.

My nanny and grandad toot to me in their little red car,
I can see a red, white and yellow police car slowly turning the corner,
I hear birds happily singing away above the treetops.

I hear the sound of metal clanging together as people are working hard in the garage,
I can smell exhaust fumes coming from a car,
I can see cars of all shapes, sizes and colours.

Amy Lamont (9)
Beacon Hill Primary School, Hindhead

As I Slowly Walk . . .

As I slowly walk to the icy white park,
I see freezing white ice gently falling onto the brightly coloured swings,
I can hear the wind trying to make it as cold as possible.

When I look into the garden I see the leaves gently falling on the ground,
I hear the sound of beautiful birds singing in the old tree,
I can hear the sound of squirrels scurrying up a tree looking for nuts.

When I look at the blue sky it makes me feel happy,
I look up high and see little bits of white snow falling on my face,
As the soft white snow falls on my face black clouds begin to gather.

In the spring little flowers will begin to grow,
They will die slowly in the winter,
Then it will be time to buy some more beautiful flowers.

Kelly McMahon (9)
Beacon Hill Primary School, Hindhead

During My Day

There are people walking the path,
They stop to talk to some friends,
I think they are enjoying themselves talking with each other.

My body is frozen,
I am shivering with cold,
I feel like an ice cube.

The smell of food makes me hungry,
My tummy has started to rumble,
I need food.

The pictures in the shop are very arty,
Bright colours,
Yellow, red, blue and green.

There are lots of green leaves,
But also different colours alike;
Orange, red, yellow and of course, green.

Amy Jackson (8)
Beacon Hill Primary School, Hindhead

The Classroom Was Crazy Because . . .

The books were banging in the bookcase
The homework hated Hollie
The spellings were spitting at Samuel
The glasses were glowing in the gutter
The pencil was pinging all over the place
The pens were patient for me to use them
The sharpener was slimy and silky
The whiteboard was wiping the windows
The computer was coming
The stapler smelt of salmon
The dry wipe pen was dripping with ink

And then in walked the head!

Sam De St Croix (8)
Beacon Hill Primary School, Hindhead

In My Day

I heard the birds tweeting in the trees
I think they are singing to each other
I think they are singing Busted

I saw a bird's nest high in a tree
I hope they'll all be OK because
It's windy and cold
So let's hope they're warm and
They're cosy

I hear an electric saw and it's very noisy
I hope he's OK, there are sparks that can
Catch fire

I see some soggy logs
They are in an overgrown hedge
Wet leaves are underneath.

Richard Cowdery (9)
Beacon Hill Primary School, Hindhead

I Can See . . .

I see a video shop with different colours
The army shop is different colours
And the rocket launcher is green

I see a car go past fast
Down the road
The car is going so fast because he was in a rush

I feel really warm because I am rubbing my hands
When I am woken I feel cold
I feel cold because the wind is a bit strong.

Jason Ayling (9)
Beacon Hill Primary School, Hindhead

Trinidad

On an island far away,
We had a lovely holiday.

With coconuts
And little huts.

With warm sea
And wild animals with fleas.

The sun was hot,
The sky was clear.

We had fun on the beach,
But I had sand flies buzzing around my ear.

We also saw cocoa pods
And men with fishing rods.

To finish off the holiday,
We had a nice long play!

Natalie Whiten (9)
Beaufort Primary School, Woking

Snakes

Snakes always hiss
When they spit, they sometimes miss
They move around in a strange way
That makes them slow in the day
They bite with all their might
That's why people always get a fright
They leap up in the air
Like they don't care
Rattlesnakes nest
Their sounds are always a pest.

Ross Green (9)
Beaufort Primary School, Woking

Sun, Sun, Sun!

One night I watched the sun go down,
It was an awesome sight,
But the sudden coming of the dark,
Gave me an awful fright.

One night I watched the sun go down,
In a pink and yellow sky,
It was such a gorgeous thing,
I cried, 'Oh my, oh my!'

One morn I watched the sun rise up,
Behind the tall, green trees,
It was a gorgeous sight to see,
I fell upon my knees.

One morn I watched the sun rise up,
In the pale blue sky,
The early birds were calling out,
With their musical cries.

The sun, the sun,
The sun, the sun,
Beautiful at all
Times.

The sun, the sun,
The sun, the sun,
Will brighten up
All lives.

Rosie Cranie-Higgs (10)
Beaufort Primary School, Woking

Things I Like And Hate

I like climbing trees
I like riding bikes
But best of all I really like
Flying kites

I like eating biscuits
I like eating sweets
But best of all I really like
Eating lots of meat

I hate cleaning my room
I hate going to bed
But worst of all I really hate
Cleaning out the shed

I hate eating sprouts
I hate eating peas
But worst of all I really hate
Cauliflower cheese.

Katie Franklyn (10)
Beaufort Primary School, Woking

Poems

Poems are very good to read
I think they're really clever,
But when I have to write one
It seems to take forever.

Should they rhyme or shouldn't they?
Should they be a riddle?
Finding rhyming words is OK
But what can I write in the middle?

Linzi Davidson (10)
Beaufort Primary School, Woking

My Family Are Completely Nuts!

My family are completely nuts,
You should see the things we do,
It must run in my genes or blood,
'Cos I'm pretty mad too.

My family are completely nuts,
Especially my nan,
She has always been like this,
But I love my groovy gran.

My family are completely nuts,
It's just the way we are,
Everything we do or say,
Turns out to sound so bizarre.

My family are completely nuts,
Both my parents are just plain mad,
My mum acts like a young, bonny lass
And my dad like a young lad.

My family are completely nuts,
But they are a part of me,
Never would I change a thing
About my family tree.

Carly Baker (10)
Beaufort Primary School, Woking

Through The Woods

Running through the woods,
Staring at all the green trees,
Blinded by the sun.

Finding all the birds,
On the ground, looking for worms,
Diving in for fish.

James Hopper (11)
Beaufort Primary School, Woking

Me And My Best Friend

You may think I am mad,
Or even sad,
For my friend
Has a weird trend,
He's a special case,
For he has no face.

For my friend
He can bend!
He can disappear without a trace,
But if that's the case,
He does not like the dark,
So he does not go to the park.

Most people think I am mad
Or even sad,
For my friend
Has a weird trend,
Can you guess who he is?
Yes, of course, he's my shadow.

Amanda Lyons (11)
Beaufort Primary School, Woking

Flowers

Roses are pretty
Bluebells are handsome
God made them all
Daisies are soft
Dandelions are yellow
God made the Earth
Poppies are tremendous
Sunflowers are bright like the sun in the sky
And God loves us all
Violets are soft with the world's greatest joy
God made them all.

Rebecca Hare (9)
Beaufort Primary School, Woking

Seasons

Spring is when the days get warmer
And plants and trees start to grow
Daffodils and tulips pop their heads up
And make our gardens all aglow

Summer is the warmest season
The days are nice and bright
Time to go on holiday
And enjoy the summer sight

In autumn the days get shorter
And the leaves begin to fall
Birds fly to a warmer country
And the farmers harvest the corn

Winter is the coldest time of year
When snow and frost appear
This is when we wrap up warm
To keep us in good cheer.

Nicholas Savage (10)
Beaufort Primary School, Woking

The Sea

What lies beneath the deep blue sea?
I wonder if a dolphin will swim with me?
So many colours and fishes galore
I wonder if they'll get washed up onto the shore?
Maybe a mermaid swimming below
Her beautiful scales she'll love to show
Sea horses seaweed and starfish too
All live beneath the sea so blue.

Hannah Doe (9)
Beaufort Primary School, Woking

Pets

I have a pet rabbit, her ears are all floppy,
She has a spotty tail and a spotty face,
She even looks like Mr Blobby.

My friend has a pet mouse and his name is Squeak,
He has a girlfriend called Bubbles,
She likes to play hide-and-seek.

My cousin has a smart cat, she looks as sweet as candy,
But she is very clever,
She invented something quite handy.

My brother has a pet parrot,
He is teaching him to talk,
He can say toast, towel, train and tea
And his newest word is fork.

My nan has a little turtle,
His head is as small as a nut,
At night you might hear a tut tut,
Because he is making himself a hut.

Lucy Hockin (9)
Beaufort Primary School, Woking

Granny's Cooking

My granny loves to do the cooking
Biscuits, cakes and yummy puddings,
When we visit she often bakes,
Sometimes yummy chocolate cakes.

Some are big, some are small,
But Granny's cakes taste best of all,
Some have cream, some have fruit,
But all of them will make you . . . smile.

Paul Dawson (9)
Beaufort Primary School, Woking

Seasons

In winter it snows
So get some hot chocolate
And warm up your toes

It is spring now
Not too cold
Only a little bit warm
All the baby animals are being born

Come on, now it's the warmest season
Now I can play with my friend, Steven
Let's go in the shade with lemonade

It is autumn now
Don't forget
We cannot watch the sun set.

Laura Henry (9)
Beaufort Primary School, Woking

Who Am I?

My first is in bark but not in woof,
My second is in hand but not in hoof,
My third is in tree but not in wood,
My fourth is in naughty but not in good,
My fifth is in mist but not in fog,
My sixth is in twig but not in log,
My seventh is in mum but not in dad,
My eighth is in happy but not in sad,
My ninth is in shirt but not in tie,
My tenth is in nose but not in eye,
My last is in flan but not in pie.
Who am I?

Bart Simpson.

Max Rodgers (11)
Beaufort Primary School, Woking

The Theme Park

We love going to the theme park,
We stay there till dark,
We try to get on every ride,
There is even a park,
We go to the pool sometimes
And go on all the slides,
The annoying thing about the pool
Has to be the tides.

The park is full of adventures,
The best thing about it is the monkey bars,
Sometimes there are bands there,
They play guitars.

The best ride out of the lot
Has to be Colossus,
But you know what it makes me feel like,
It makes me feel so nauseous.
Well, that's my poem,
I hope you enjoyed it,
Maybe you can go to the theme park,
I know you will enjoy that.

Charlotte Miles (10)
Beaufort Primary School, Woking

Yummy In My Tummy

Peter likes peppers on pizza
And Chelsea likes candy and chocolate,
Jessie eats jelly and jam,
While Lucy licks lemons and lollies,
Ben buys crunchy biscuits
And Mike grows munchy melons,
Steven sips Sainsbury's soda,
While Muffy munches chocolate chip muffins.

Lucy Colleer (9)
Beaufort Primary School, Woking

The Changing Seasons

Spring
Spring is joyful and exciting,
Birds are singing with delight,
So many trees in bloom together,
What a truly magnificent sight!

Summer
Summer is so colourful,
With all the different flowers,
Because it is so nice and warm,
The children play outside for hours and hours!

Autumn
Autumn has such different colours,
So many trees turn to gold,
The parks and gardens look warm and glowing,
But soon it will be winter and starting to get cold!

Winter
Now that it is winter
We really can feel the cold,
Don't forget to wrap up warm,
Remember, you've been told!

Jennifer Cross (10)
Beaufort Primary School, Woking

Adam's School Days

S cience is great, science is fun, everybody knows it
   because it's full of fun
C hildren love to have some fun with their friends
   and with their mum
H ello teacher, what's our lesson today?
O f all my lessons, maths is my favourite thing
O ur friends love to sing
L ucky are we, our teacher is great, we never want to be late.

Adam Youlton (9)
Beaufort Primary School, Woking

My Trip To The Zoo

When I went to the zoo an . . .

    A lligator snarled at me, a
    B aboon just stared at me, a
    C rocodile snapped at me and a
    D ingo barked at me.

    E lephants trumpeted at me, a
    F ish blew bubbles at me, a
    G iraffe galloped up to me and a
    H orse neighed at me.

    I nsects bit me, a
    J aguar chased me, a
    K oala hugged me and a
    L ion roared at me.

    M onkeys laughed at me, a
    N ightingale sang to me, an
    O ctopus nearly strangled me and a
    P elican pecked me.

    Q uails flew away from me, a
    R abbit jumped up at my legs, a
    S nake tried to bite me, but a
    T ortoise just stared gormlessly.

A   U nicorn let me ride on her back, a
    V ulture squawked at me, a
    W hale flapped its tail at me and a
Fo X crept up on me.

    Y awning, I was just about to shut my eyes when I saw a stripy
    Z ebra crossing the road!

Indeera Shankla (8)
Beaufort Primary School, Woking

Holiday

Holidays, holidays I love you
Holidays, holidays bring the canoe
Let's go down to the sea today
Mum can sleep and we can play

We can go in the caravan
Please make it hot, don't forget the fan
At the pool there will be lots of slides
And at the fair there will be lots of rides

You eat loads of yummy food
And hang out with all the top dudes
See all of the pantomimes
And have lots of great, great times

But at the end
Don't forget to send
A big postcard
To all your friends!

Samuel Exworth (10)
Beaufort Primary School, Woking

When I Was

When I was one I sucked my thumb,
When I was two I licked my shoe,
When I was three I climbed a tree,
When I was four we got a new floor,
When I was five I learnt to drive,
When I was six I fell in a ditch
When I was seven I went to Devon
When I was eight I got up late
When I was nine I made a chime
When I was ten I bought a pen.

Natalie Tunnell (8)
Beaufort Primary School, Woking

The Seasons

Spring
Spring is nice,
When all the mice
Come out at night,
To give you a fright.

Summer
Everything has grown,
Where new lambs roam,
Trees have leaves,
Blowing in the breeze.

Autumn
There are leaves on the floor,
When I open the door,
There are no colours around,
Because everywhere is brown.

Winter
There is snow around
And all over the ground,
A white sheet covers the lake,
So everybody can skate.

Mitchell Rogers (10)
Beaufort Primary School, Woking

My Dog, Kassie

She's big and hairy,
But oh what a fairy.
She's over 8 stone
And as thick as a bone.
She's a dustbin on legs,
When you eat, she begs.
A slobbery big lassie,
That's my dog, Kassie!

Zoe Wright (10)
Beaufort Primary School, Woking

My World

Come into my head,
To my imagination,
Where all is able.

Where you can fly around the world
And have super strength
And you are invincible.

Where you can be tall
Or any colour you want,
Or be anything.

You have super speed
And have magic whenever,
Metal creatures

Shoot beams from your bodies,
Shoot laser beams
And eat all the food you want.

So now leave my mind,
Because it will never come true,
So that's the end, bye.

Christopher James (10)
Beaufort Primary School, Woking

My Poem

She's big, she's hairy but not a fairy,
Go in the town with her crown,
She's big as a pig,
But she does have a dig,
She has long hair
And she is quite rare.

She is my dog, but looks like a log,
She's on her own and eats a bone
And she's my dog, nine-year-old Jimmy.

Jade Mitchell (10)
Beaufort Primary School, Woking

When I Walked Down The Street

When I walked down the street
I caught a beat
And this is the way it went

People greet
When they meet
When I walked down the street

Children at school
Acting cool
When I walked down the street

The flowers were blooming
The ladies were grooming
When I walked down the street

Children were crying
Mums sighing
When I walked down the street

The lamps were glowing
The wind was blowing
When I walked down the street

The night was dark
I heard a lark
When I walked down the street

I opened the door
Now it's a bore
When I had walked down the street.

Nathanael Osborne (10)
Beaufort Primary School, Woking

The Wrong Holiday!

When you go on holiday everyone is glad
Except from when your £1.50 ice cream
Goes *splat* on the ground,
You get another one and the same happens again,
Either you have butter fingers
Or you're completely round the bend!

You told me your apartment wasn't bad,
Apart from all the bugs that were crawling on your hands!

Your bed sounded great except from you broke it
And was paid out of your money
(A lot of it!)

Well, it sounded quite a good holiday in lovely Spain,
Apart from your mum told me you were a really big
Pain!

Jemma Percy (10)
Beaufort Primary School, Woking

What Was That?

What was that?
I hear you say,
Is it the wind
By the window?
No.

But what was it?
Do you *really* want to know?
Yes, it was that monster that lives under your bed,
Yes it is that monster that wants to have your head.

But do not worry,
You are starting to fret,
He only comes out when he is in debt!

Lewis Jones (11)
Beaufort Primary School, Woking

If I Win . . .

Have you heard about the poem competition?
An entry form I've found,
It says here in the small print,
First prize is twenty pounds!

I've thought about this carefully,
I think I'll have a bash,
I've already thought of the books I could buy,
If I win the cash!

I might choose Harry Potter,
Sabrina gets a tick,
The book called 'Triplets' does sound fun,
There's just so many to pick!

'Fairy Dust' and 'The Mum Hunt',
Two books by Gwyneth Rees,
Poems by Spike Milligan,
I could choose one of these!

What happens if I don't win,
It wouldn't be so great,
It has to be done perfectly,
My entry can't be late!

I'd have to wash up all the dishes
And iron all my gear,
To earn all this money,
It would take me almost a year!

Emily Hopper (10)
Beaufort Primary School, Woking

The Variety Of Life

The butterfly flies swiftly and silently soaring up into the sky.
The bumblebee buzzes through the hive making honey
                                              for people to eat.
The kingfisher dives into the water to catch fish for tea.
The zebra gallops across the plains in the hot summer sun.
The dolphin skims the glimmering sea making waves
                                          as he races his friends.

Zoe Richardson (10)
Beaufort Primary School, Woking

The Frosty Winter

W inter is wonderful, it's so nice to see
I t's nice and snowy and as pretty as can be
N ow let's go and build a snowman, come on, you and me
T he icy lakes and frosty grass, it crackles in your footsteps
E xciting snow with snowball fights with nice warm beds to snuggle
R ainy sometimes but fun as well to watch the lovely raindrops fall.

Stephanie Withers (9)
Beaufort Primary School, Woking

Sports

S wimming is exercise,
P ool is fun,
O bstacle course to test your stamina,
R owing to build your muscles,
T ae kwon do is a martial art,
S kateboarding is to test your skills of balance.

Rebecca McVeigh (11)
Beaufort Primary School, Woking

The Four Seasons

Spring
    S o many trees and flowers in bloom
    P roud of the spring, the birds sing out
    R ound are the nests that they create
    I n the nest the young birds chirp
    N ow that is a welcome sound
    G ood is the season called spring

Summer
    S o good it is to see the sun
    U p in the sky so warm and bright
    M mm is the ice cream while it lasts
    M elting in the heat so fast
    E verything is warm and hot
    R arely does our playtime stop

Autumn
    A utumn is nice with all the trees
    U ntil the leaves come off
    T hen the cold winds blow
    U mbrellas you may need
    M aybe scarves and gloves as well
    N ow is the time to walk and play

Winter
    W hat we do not need are shorts
    I think that winter coats are best
    N o more leaves are on the trees
    T hen Christmas time is coming near
    E ver joyful with good cheer
    R oaring fires with food and beer.

Chloe Mackay (11)
Beaufort Primary School, Woking

My Favourite Sports!

Here comes the ball,
While my friends are at the mall,
I am very tall,
Just like a wall.

I like tennis
And my brother's called Dennis
And also a right menace,
That's why I like tennis.

I like swimming,
Although I'm always winning,
I go every week,
Which is on a Saturday.

I like cricket,
I stand behind a wicket,
Which I always
Get a player out on that very day.

I like basketball,
I'm always scoring goals,
Give the ball to me
And I'll score another goal.

Jade Barclay (11)
Beaufort Primary School, Woking

Life With Love

Love is like a soaring dove,
Swiftly sailing through the open spaces,
At quiet paces, making sure that one day
He will finally meet it,
The life with love that he's destined for,
The woman he loves,
Now it's springtime
And the doves now know about this sweet rhyme,
They know it's not a crime to fall in love,
The life with love.

James Hart (10)
Beaufort Primary School, Woking

My Garden

The roses are red
So I said
The blossom is pink
As I wink
Bluebells are blue
As the weather is cool

The pond is full of water
A quarter is not full of water
The weather is sunny
So here comes a bunny

The bushes are green
Always to be seen
The cat is sweet
And she likes meat.

Chloe Webb (10)
Beaufort Primary School, Woking

My Dog

I have a little dog
We take him to the park
When we play
He always seems to bark
He rolls around
And jumps up and down
All through the town
He's just a little dog
That I had found
He's all mine
My one and only hound.

Steven Shaw (8)
Beaufort Primary School, Woking

At The Seaside

One day I went to the seaside,
I went in the cool blue sea,
When I came out of the sea,
My brother threw seaweed on me.

My mum told my brother off,
But he didn't care,
So I sat down on the beach
And ate a juicy pear.

I ate all the juicy pears,
Then I went back in the sea,
I was having great fun,
Until I found a green pea.

I was scared,
So I went to my mum,
She wasn't listening,
Then suddenly I hurt my thumb.

Joanne Burton (10)
Beaufort Primary School, Woking

On My Way To School!

I was on my way to school,
I had a nasty fall,
I broke my leg, can't kick a ball,
So now I have to get a lift to school,
Oh, I do feel such a fool.

I now travel with my friends,
Quick, we're turning a bend,
We were going as fast as we can,
Then we crashed into a big fat man.

When I arrived at school,
I told my friends about my nasty fall
And about the man who's dead
Because we ran over his big fat head.

Luke Reed (10)
Beaufort Primary School, Woking

My Little Baby Sister

My little baby sister has red hair
She's six months old
And is cuddly like a bear
She rolls around the floor with her Winnie the Pooh
And plays with Tigger too.

My little baby sister, she's so sweet
She can even suck her feet
She goes in the bath and makes me laugh
She really is a treat.

My little baby sister
She laughs a lot and giggles
And when we put her on the floor
She does lots of wiggles.

My little baby sister
I play with her all day and
When I go to school
I miss her more than I can say.

I'm so glad I have a sister
She makes me very happy.

Katie Thorne (11)
Beaufort Primary School, Woking

My Riddle

My first is in red but not in blue
My second is in afraid but not in timid
My third is in ice but not in flame
My fourth is in no but not in yes
My fifth is in big but not in small
My sixth is in odd but not in usual
My seventh is in wet but not in dry.

Victoria Hubbard (10)
Beaufort Primary School, Woking

Football

Football is a game I like,
It is much more fun than on my bike,
You can play it at the park,
You can play it at home,
It doesn't matter where you go.

You can play it with friends,
Or on your own,
You can play it in Spain,
Or even in Rome.

The game is great,
It's lots of fun,
It makes me laugh,
It makes me run.

This is the end of my poem,
I have to go,
So now's the time to say how-de-ho!

Ryan Johnson (10)
Beaufort Primary School, Woking

What Am I?

I can be liquid,
I can be powder,
I can be bubbly too,
Some people like me,
Some people don't,
But I'm mainly lovely,
Through and through,
Some people like me warm,
Some people like me cold,
I can be in sandwiches,
I can go with apple crumble,
What am I?

Amy Horner (10)
Beaufort Primary School, Woking

Serpent

He waits patiently, that is the key,
For prey to walk by unexpectedly,
His only instinct is to survive,
That is his life.

He moves slowly through the damp, dank grass,
He stalks his victim without a sound,
His mind set on his daily task,
Slithering and sliding along the ground.

In the dead of night he strikes
And suffocates his prey,
It's murder in cold blood they say,
But that is life's way.

He slithers back into his cave,
So he goes to sleep,
To recharge and stay the night,
So he is prepared for a possible fight.

As he rests he sheds his skin,
To get a new shiny coat upon him,
He feels the chill in his lair
And ventures into the warm morning air.

Crawling through the undergrowth,
He is challenged by a fearsome beast,
The battle fought was long and hard,
But the mongoose had a lovely feast.

The only part that now remains
Is the dead skin in the cave.

Alexander Edwards (10)
Beaufort Primary School, Woking

Shopping

I hate going shopping with my mum and dad,
They drag me down the aisles saying,
'No, you can't have that!'
'Why Mum? Please Mum, my friend takes it in her lunch
You're so mean Mum, let me have a munch.'

She makes me go down the veggie aisle,
Making me look like a wally,
This is the only aisle I won't put anything in her trolley.

I wander down to the CDs,
It's the highlight of the shop,
I still hate going shopping,
Whether the music is jazz, rock or pop.

We arrive at the checkout,
Put our shopping on the belt,
The lady starts chatting
And I just want to get *out!*

Ella Vickers (10)
Beaufort Primary School, Woking

Our Polluted World

The number of cars continue to grow,
The fumes damage the atmosphere we all know.

Lots of chemicals run into rivers,
The thought of the fish dying makes me shiver.

Out at sea there are oil slicks
And when I think of them it makes me feel sick.

Even when we just come inside after play,
Our clothes smell bad and we hope the smell won't stay.

Pollution is damaging the world today
And I think one day we'll have to pay.

Robert Whiten (10)
Beaufort Primary School, Woking

Seasons Of The Year

It is winter now and I think it is a bit too cold to have a snowball fight,
So let's get in and fill our tummies with a Christmas din!

And now it's spring and all the plants and animals are growing!
So the sun is up and if we have enough luck, we can go to
                                                        the ice cream shop!

And so summer is near and let's not have any fear in going
                                                        for a swim!
So jump into the pond and you should feel cool!

Autumn is here so come out and have autumn fun!
So come and listen to the swishing leaves and jump around!

Rebecca Lee (8)
Beaufort Primary School, Woking

Snow, Rain, Sun

I like the sun because it's warm
and there's lost of fun things to be done!

I like the rain falling on my head
but some people would rather be in bed!

I like the snowflakes falling from the sky
but some people would rather eat yummy pie!

Jasmin Pilott (10)
Beaufort Primary School, Woking

Fireworks

First we let off the rockets,
Whizz, fizz, bang!
Then we light the sparklers,
They sound like scrunching up paper,
We see the last fireworks
And they go off with a *crash!*

Liam Varndell (8)
Beaufort Primary School, Woking

Dragons

In the night
These creatures fly
They burn down our towns
They live in dark places
Strike when you least suspect it
As they fly they will strike with their
Burning fire-breath

They fly in the dark, dark nights
Cold, cold nights
Feel something very hot then
Run for your life
Seriously

Do not battle them
You're risking your life
Fighting the creature
It is not worth your life
Unstoppable
Uncontrollable
For this thing is a
Dragon.

Adam Tolfrey (10)
Beaufort Primary School, Woking

The Flaky Cake

My mum made me a cake, it was really flaky,
It was a chocolate cake,
It stuck to the roof of my mouth,
In fact it stuck to the roof of the house,
It was quite a big cake actually,
Everyone in the world could have got a piece,
My whole family got a piece of it,
Though I got three pieces,
My mum made me a cake,
It was really nice,
That's why it's all gone!

Stephanie Tunnell (11)
Beaufort Primary School, Woking

What Am I?

Tall and dark
My hat stands
On my sphere-like head.

Hard and shiny, I
Am the eyes.

Orange and pointy,
I stand for the
Nose.

Beady and black, I form a smile.

I have a long, multicoloured
Woollen scarf, all soft and cosy.

I have a big cold belly,
To finish me off add some arms and gloves
To keep me warm and snug.

When the sun comes up and it starts getting hot
All that will be left of me will
Be a puddle of water.

What am I?

Snowman.

Charlotte Hewett (11)
Beaufort Primary School, Woking

When In Heaven

When I die
In Heaven I'll lie,
With an angel next to me
And there I'll lay, in a coffin grey
And forever I will be.

All my happy memories
Will still be here with me,
While I'm still lying in this coffin,
With an angel next to me.

Hannah-Louise Bryan (10)
Beaufort Primary School, Woking

Dance

It's the one thing in life that makes me feel me
I can be creative, I can just let it be

Like a bird, I am free to do what I please
The chance to dance I quickly seize

My mind soars the world and out of space
And I dance in costumes covered in lace

I can be a mermaid swimming in the sea
Or a clown in a show, extremely funny

I could dance all night, dance all day
Whatever the weather I'll do what you say

Come with me, dance with me, come on, let's go
We can twirl and run, we can do a show

Who am I when I dance? Is the question here
I am not me, I'm someone else running free from fear

The enchantment, the magic, all this I enhance
When I am someone else locked in a world of *dance.*

Carla Fox (10)
Beaufort Primary School, Woking

My Mum Loves Shoes

Hundreds of pairs, new shoes, old shoes,
Shoes of many colours, blue shoes, white shoes,
Green shoes, red shoes, black shoes,
Down the high street, shop, shop, shop,
Why does she have to get more shoes?
Buckled shoes, flat shoes, comfy shoes,
Silly shoes, wacky shoes, multicoloured shoes,
Daft shoes, noisy shoes,
How many more shoes?
Shop till you drop shoes,
Please Mum, no more shoes!

Kellie Murray (11)
Beaufort Primary School, Woking

Backwards Adventure

I had an adventure last night in my dream,
But nothing was what it seemed,
Light was dark and dark was light,
The creatures came out all through the night.

Life was turned upside down,
Although I spoke I heard no sound,
The beaches had no stones nor sand,
You walked along the sky rather than land.

The queen was poor, the peasants were rich
And politely mannered was the witch,
My mum and dad went to school,
But still managed to act uncool.

Everyone walked on their hands,
For some reason this was thought very grand,
At the beginning of my dream I was sixty,
By the end of my dream I was scarcely three.

I slept in a stable, the horses were in my bed,
It is said, if you sleep in a bed, you would end up dead,
I even got to drive a car,
The thing is I didn't get very far, (I crashed).

Chelsea Reilly (10)
Beaufort Primary School, Woking

Flowers

Flowers come in different colours, red, blue and many more,
Flowers come in different types, roses, daisies and lots more,
Flowers come in different sizes, long and thin, short and fat,
Petals on flowers are smooth, sleek and also colourful.

Now the day ends, cold and raining,
As you look out the window you will see raindrops
Trickling down the flowers' stems.

Adam Dyson (11)
Beaufort Primary School, Woking

My Ladybug

There was a poorly ladybug,
It only had one leg
And when it tried to walk along,
It kept falling on its head.

Why do we call them ladybirds,
When they could be a man,
Maybe they're transsexual,
Oh, I don't understand.

It did manage to take off,
Through the air it goes,
But when it came back in to land,
It grazed up all its nose.

Because its undercarriage
Had problems coming down,
Oh, look there goes the other leg,
It's buried in the ground.

Rachel Bell (10)
Beaufort Primary School, Woking

A Little White Lie

This little white lie was not meant to hurt
Like a little white snowball
It was meant as a giggle
This little white lie rolled on and on
Like a little white snowball
Getting bigger and bigger
Picking up stones and picking up litter
So now this little white lie is 6 foot 2
It is going to hurt whoever it hits
So my advice to you is don't tell that lie
Don't throw that snowball
Don't make them cry.

Elliott Reed (10)
Beaufort Primary School, Woking

Alien

I climb into my spaceship
And whizz off in the sky
Oh, I can't believe it
I can really fly!

I go past the planets
And the Milky Way
Oh how I wish I could see this
Every single day!

And finally I arrive there
The mysterious planet Mars
And out came the aliens
Shaped like Mars bars

With the landscape so rocky
And the sky so red
I suddenly jumped up
And then I said:
'Alien!'

Hadiyah Khan (11)
Beaufort Primary School, Woking

My Sister

My annoying big sister is a pain
Sometimes she drives me insane
She dresses up all frilly
And acts oh so silly
She shouts a lot
About that spot
She is far too old for toys
But instead she goes out with boys
But when I'm blue and feeling down
She takes me out to town
She buys me sweets and lots of treats
And yummy scrummy things to eat.

Andrew Cruttenden (10)
Beaufort Primary School, Woking

Spine With Fingers

The old silent tree,
Lying in the same place day and night,
On its own,
You go in the middle and
Crunch!
Seems like you've stepped on crisps.

Spiders crawl up your back,
Feels like you're in a huge ice cube,
You shiver and wobble all about,
Keep on thinking about ghosts.

The leaves fallen off in the past years,
Lying there,
The tree wants to move,
It even says I want to move,
You can hear it speaking to you,
The noise of the rustling leaves

And now a hundred years have gone by,
You can't do anything,
So silent and calmly,
It will lay for evermore.

Mohmina Atique (10)
Beaufort Primary School, Woking

The Fighter
(Inspired by 'The Highwayman' by Alfred Noyes)

The wind was a screaming damsel,
The moon was a pirate longboat,
The road was a shimmering river
And the fighter came riding, riding, riding,
The fighter came riding up to the enemy's den.

With his visor down hiding his face,
New shining armour twinkling in the moonlight
A dark figure illuminated by the moon.

Amy Akerman (9)
Grand Avenue Primary School, Surbiton

The Lonely House!

The lonely house stood endlessly on the wood
As the hungry wolves yelped,
And a flock of bats flew above
Carrying a dead man's skull.
And out of the house came a ghost
Named Fred the garden keeper,
And at the stroke of midnight
The house quietly moved away.
So when you've found it once
You may never find it again,
In the whistling wind
The broken floorboards creak.
As the flickering candlelight
Went out in a puff of smoke,
Everything went dark and black
As the moon was hidden by clouds.

Joel Bamber (10)
Grand Avenue Primary School, Surbiton

The Old, Forbidden, Lonely House

At the old, forbidden, lonely house
A deathly ghost glided slowly by
And the howling wind whistled by
And got lost in the cloudy mists,
The floorboards creaked inside the house,
Though there was nobody there,
The flickering candlelight that glowed in the window,
Was the only light for miles
At the old, forbidden, lonely house.

Samuel Hopkins (10)
Grand Avenue Primary School, Surbiton

The Listener
(Based on 'The Listeners' by Walter De La Mare)

'Is there anybody there called the listener?'
Standing in the misty moor
He walked back round to the other side
And noticed a wooden door
He stared at the night's sudden atmosphere
And ranted at the starry sky
Then he looked at the door closely
With a sparkle in his eye.

'I'll be back later with a hammer
And wooden sphere
These ghosts are not so far
And I am not too near.'

Rio Edwin (10)
Grand Avenue Primary School, Surbiton

The Traveller
(Based on 'The Listeners' by Walter De La Mare)

'Are you there?' said a traveller
Knocking gently at the door

There was a sound of wind
Blowing strongly above the trees
And the branches whooshing
Back and forward
The leaves tumbling through the grass

'Are you there?' said the traveller
Shouting and knocking on the door strongly
But no one answered
So the traveller got back to his home
And did not come again.

Ji Weon Park (9)
Grand Avenue Primary School, Surbiton

The Traveller
(Based on 'The Listeners' by Walter De La Mare)

'Open up,' whispered the traveller,
Tapping on the dusty floor.
A hound only replying to her questions,
Howls echoing through the moor.

Once again the traveller knocked,
This time on the window.
She peered inside and all she could see
Was a burning and blazing fire.

'Open up,' she shouted,
Dusty windows swaying to and fro.
A puff of smoke came out of the chimney
Making the traveller cough.

A hideous laugh then filled the air,
As an owl glided past the moon.
The traveller looked around and scurried away,
Out of the rusty gates.

The dancing leaves swayed about
As the traveller ran away,
The traveller ran as fast as she could,
Never to be seen again.

Gaayathiri Luhinthiran (9)
Grand Avenue Primary School, Surbiton

The Pirates
(Inspired by 'The Highwayman' by Alfred Noyes)

The wind was a silent cry with nothing left to blow,
The moon was a floating boat trying hard to row,
The sea was a still river with not a wave
And the pirate ship came sailing, sailing, sailing,
The pirate ship came sailing up to the big black cave.

Jackson Tyler (10)
Grand Avenue Primary School, Surbiton

The Highwayman

'Let me in, let me in,' bellowed the highwayman
As the red coats came near
And he clambered into the house
And the shutters banged and creaked
As the red coats marched nearer and nearer
His heart was pounding hard
And the red coats broke the door down
But he had gone.

Alexander Hazzard (9)
Grand Avenue Primary School, Surbiton

The Highwayman
(Inspired by 'The Highwayman' by Alfred Noyes)

The wind was a howling wolf of sorrow,
The moon was a ghostly face,
The road was a roller coaster twisting this way and that
And the highwayman came trotting,
Trotting, trotting,
The highwayman came trotting up to the old inn door.

Alice Brace (10)
Grand Avenue Primary School, Surbiton

The Highwayman
(Based on 'The Highwayman' by Alfred Noyes)

The wind was a cold, howling beast
The moon was a ghostly skull drifting in the sky
The road was a never-ending stream of darkness
And the highwayman came trotting, trotting, trotting
The highwayman came trotting up to the old inn door.

Joshua Nicholls (10)
Grand Avenue Primary School, Surbiton

The Traveller
(Based on 'The Listeners' by Walter De La Mare)

'Open up!' shouted the traveller,
Knocking on the old inn door
And his horse remained tied up by a tree,
Drinking from the nearby moor.

And a black cat shot out of the window,
Past the traveller's legs,
Under the tied up horse,
Into a fern-like hedge.

And the traveller shouted and shouted again,
But silence answered his call,
Although the traveller heard footsteps,
Creeping through the hall.

He waited for what seemed years,
Every second crawling by,
But no one answered his door to see him,
No one answered his cry.

Katie Legg (10)
Grand Avenue Primary School, Surbiton

The Strange Traveller
(Based on 'The Listeners' by Walter De La Mare)

'Is there anybody there?' wailed the traveller,
Kicking on the wooden door
And rustling leaves were falling
Onto the forest floor,
Dusty windows shaken by the fierce wind
And heavy rain rippling on the tree branches,
'Is there anybody there?' screamed the traveller,
Punching on the wooden door.

Kiran Gurmail (10)
Grand Avenue Primary School, Surbiton

Lady Of The Light

Staying at the old haunted hotel
By the seashore, stood the visitor
He'd been there before
But came back to explore
He'd heard of the ghostly lady of the light
Who made people take flight
She wore a long cloak of white
And she gave him quite a fright
She no longer wanted to scare
So smiled and waved goodbye
To the lonely visitor just standing there.

James Taylor (10)
Grand Avenue Primary School, Surbiton

The Slow Sunrise

The slow but bright sunrise drifted up to the sky
The phantom's house glowed but inside it stayed dark
In the far, misty dance the ghost's daughter started to cry
She saw a human but he could not see her
In the dark, spooky house the mother started to make human brain
Dirty old toenails, rabbits' sick with blood
The family enjoyed the food so she shouted
'Have more for devil's sake!'
But the phantoms stay haunted
Still they stay listening - listening - listening.

Louis Hebbs (10)
Grand Avenue Primary School, Surbiton

The Stranger

'What was that?' whispered the child
Putting the storybook down.
He heard the wind howling,
As the creaky windows rattled.
Knock, knock, knock on the wooden door,
As the child crept quietly towards it,
He hid quickly behind the bookshelf
Waiting for a call,
Then it came, a small low grunt,
'Can I come in?'
Someone was there,
Knocking at the door.
The terrified child held his breath,
Waiting for the old door to kick open.
But it didn't, instead there were footsteps,
They were getting quieter,
Whoever it was, never returned.

Kajaniy Kannapiran (10)
Grand Avenue Primary School, Surbiton

The Ghost's House

The old, gloomy house stands in the dark, gloomy forest
And the howling wind raced past swishing the trees,
As the candle started flickering.

The ghosts wake up, oooooh-oooooh
And the owl begins hooting, tu-whit, tu-whoo,
As the ghosts go back to bed
And the candle is blown out.

Maya Randhawa (9)
Grand Avenue Primary School, Surbiton

When Snow Falls

When snow falls
I would get out and play
When the day comes
There are a few, there are a few things to play
Among the snow
Why not try and build a castle
Or maybe you can build a snowman
But only if you're good
Come on and play in the snow today
Go sledging down the hill
Sledging is great
It's super-duper
After a cold, snowy winter's day
Have a nice hot warm drink
But don't stop now
You've got tomorrow
That means more fun
Yeah!
We're going to have more fun.

John Caklais (7)
Lodge School, Purley

The Nasty Dragon

'Arrgghh!' I shouted
The dragon
The dragon roaring like mad
I could smell his deadly mouth
On the hills above
I was climbing up
With my sword and shield
Holding my nose
To get away from the stench.

Preten Patel (8)
Lodge School, Purley

50th Anniversary

Oh how I love glorious Wales,
With its beautiful countryside,
Green valleys and stony hills,
As I look out of my window
And there I see, the highest mountain,
Snowdon, gazing back at me.
Outside it suddenly starts to rain
And the sheep are looking cold and scared,
They seem to be looking for somewhere to hide,
On this cold, rainy, February day.
Most people speak English,
But some speak Welsh
And funnily enough their emblem is a leek,
I am looking forward to going home but
I will always treasure my time in Wales.

Kirsty Downing (8)
Lodge School, Purley

Rain

Rain, rain, the rain falls down
And the raindrops are splashing on the ground,
The rain is dropping on the ground,
The rain is splashing on the rooftop,
The rain is wet,
The rain is soggy,
The rain is dropping,
The rain is water,
The rain is cold,
Rain, rain, the water is splashing,
Rain, rain, the water is wet,
Rain, rain, the water is cold,
Rain, rain, the water is soggy,
Rain, rain, it's raining.

Wei-Zheng Tan (7)
Lodge School, Purley

Dustbin Dogs

Here they come
They're here again
Here come the dustbin dogs
Howling and barking
Prowling the street
Here come the dustbin dogs

Scratching doors
Chasing cats
Here come the dustbin dogs
Scavenging in plastic bags
Hunting for food
Here come the dustbin dogs.

Anna Caklais (9)
Lodge School, Purley

The Welsh Flag

The Welsh flag, red, green, white,
Red counts for fierce dragons,
Green counts for the evil grass,
White for the gloomy sky.

Hot fire comes out,
Burning flames,
People die,
Never come back.

People fight,
People die,
People try,
But they never survive.

Vishala Nadesan (8)
Lodge School, Purley

The Demon Teacher

The teacher plods the classroom
Eyes on fire
Waiting to strike
A devastating blow
Hair on fire
Like the fires of Hell
Razor-sharp teeth
And claws glinting
Here it comes
. . . and I wish I hadn't talked!

Michael Burgoyne (9)
Lodge School, Purley

November The Fifth

Rockets are red,
Catherine wheels are blue,
Bangers are noisy,
Dynamite too!
Shooting stars sparkle,
Sparklers do too,
Big kings go boom,
In green, red and blue.

Michael Cross (8)
Lodge School, Purley

Fireworks

Fireworks! Fireworks!
So light and bright!
Fireworks! Fireworks!
So mad and bad!
Fireworks! Fireworks!
So colourful and playful!

Dominic Bishop (9)
Lodge School, Purley

Get The Feeling!

It is Christmas!
Get the feeling when Christmas arrives!
Beautiful gifts and new presents!
Get the feeling!
When the Christmas tree comes
You will be surprised,
Stars come upon you
Because it's . . . Christmas time!
Dazzling sprinkles of surprised glitter
Rise upon you,
Get the feeling!
Gifts, gifts, gifts,
Wrapped up just for you
And it is Christmas time!

Yasmine Heinel (9)
Lodge School, Purley

Getting Told Off

Most of the time I get told off
Sometimes I laugh!
Other times I cry
I have to be clever so I don't get told off

What have I done to get told off?
Oh yes, I remember, annoying my sister all the time,
I always get told, the fault was mine,
I say sorry to my mum and dad,
I feel really sad because I know I have been bad!

Bilal Shariff (8)
Lodge School, Purley

Books

Books, books
I can never get books out of my head
Horror, comedy
Children's, biography
Never can I get those books out of my head!
But I like books
I like to read them
Some I hate
They are so boring
But some are exciting
I can never put them down
All books are boring
But only at the start
I like books
I hate books
I can never decide.

Lewis Phenix (10)
Lodge School, Purley

Netball Match

We're going to play netball with Collingwood,
Collingwood arrive and we start the match,
Mrs Edwards tosses the ball,
Charlotte catches the ball
And passes it to Hannah,
She shoots
And it misses,
She tries again
And she scores, yeah!
We all said well done to each other
For playing so good.

Bonnie Streeter (9)
Lodge School, Purley

Passchendaele

In a foreign field he lay,
Lonely soldier, unknown grave.
On his dying words he prays,
Tell the world of Passchendaele.

Relive all that he's been through
Rust your bullets with his tears,
Let me tell you about his years.

Laying low in a mud-filled trench,
Killing time till my very own death,
On my face,
I can feel the falling rain,
Never see my friends again.

Stand tall for the very last time,
Guns ready as I stand in line,
Wait for the whistle to blow,
Rush of blood and over we go.

See my spirit on the wind,
Over the lines, beyond the hills,
Friend and foe will meet again,
Those who died at Passchendaele.

Kian Bagheri (10)
Lodge School, Purley

Rainbow

Rainbow, rainbow, it's so colourful
It is red, black, blue, orange and purple
It goes in the sky
With stars in the night

Big and
Strong rainbow
And when it's sunny and rainy
The colours come out of the rainbow.

Joshua Green (9)
Lodge School, Purley

Cold

It's winter
Oh no
I'm very, very cold
What do I do?
I need warmth
But I now live on the streets
What do I do?
All I have is this thin top
And these light shorts
Won't anybody help me . . . ?
I'm so sad and very cold
I'm hungry
I've no food
Or drink
Or money
Or anything
It's like Hell in the cold
I'm sobbing
Sobbing for my mum
I've gone without food
For a week
I can feel my life slipping away
I can't feel the cold
Or the pain anymore.

Kane Rodney (9)
Lodge School, Purley

Sports

Sport is lots of people's favourite thing
Most people like football
Lots of dads like rugby
But I like golf
It's a gentle, fun game
I don't play in tournaments
I just play for fun.

Alexander Viveash (10)
Lodge School, Purley

Hellfire

Hell! Hell! Hell!
The flame licked the oily scales of the Welsh beast
A screech!
A scream!
A crash!
Smoke engulfed the whole anatomy
A shadow keeled over
Another beast lumbered out of its dwelling
A shallow cave littered with filth
It's hair!
Oh the hair!
It looked like the fires of Hell!
Then I was engulfed in smoke
I know no more!

James Weber (10)
Lodge School, Purley

The Best Day Of My Life

It's the best day of my life!
I am going to see a cricket match,
I can't wait,
It will be so cool.
The match is India vs Australia,
I'll pack my lunch,
I'll take my pen and paper
To get signatures,
Money to buy a special bat,
'Dad, which seat are we sitting in?'
'The first row!'
'Woo-hoo!'

Sachin Duggal (8)
Lodge School, Purley

Football Crazy!

Yeah, come on Wales!
Score one more try to win the game!
. . . Yes!
Go Wales - go Wales,
We have won the cup,
The World Cup!
Celebration time, come on,
You open the champagne . . .
You start cooking . . .
We are going to have a feast.

Andrew Ovenden (9)
Lodge School, Purley

The Dragon Flag Of Wales

The Welsh flag,
The different colours it has,
Red, white and green and a dragon hungry and mean,
Green crusty scales,
Sharp teeth like knives
And one long tail with a point of a sword,
Long ears
And a head that is bold.

David Omonya (10)
Lodge School, Purley

School

S chool is fantastic
C lasswork is fun
H istory a lesson
O n weekdays we come
O ur teacher helps us every day
L unchtime comes, we're out to play.

Johanna Baird (8)
St Dunstan's CE Primary School, Cheam

I Went To Devon

I went to Devon last year
With my friends of course

We stayed up late
Till midnight I think

Then Felix started telling stories
Ghost stories!

Then he stopped, he fell asleep
In mid-sentence

But me and Rowan didn't
We saw something move

Arrgghh!
It was Mum

Phew!

But there is proof we saw a ghost
He left a note next to Felix's
Head!

Evie Hunter Bell (9)
St Dunstan's CE Primary School, Cheam

A Night-Time Stroll

My brother told a story
A really scary story

I took a night-time stroll
A long night-time stroll

An owl hooted loudly
An owl hooted really loudly

The trees looked like men
The trees looked like moving men

I ran back home
I ran quickly home.

Jacob Watt (8)
St Dunstan's CE Primary School, Cheam

The Dragon

Lying on piles of gold,
Watching bats fly around,
He's fought knights in the days of old,
Now he's ancient and can't hear a sound!

Wearing rings,
Crowns,
And other things,
He frowns!

He gloomily sings,
'When I was young
I had loads of fun
And I could do many things

But now I'm old
I'm not as strong
I have lived for centuries too long.'
And then he was gone.

Matthew Blackman (9)
St Dunstan's CE Primary School, Cheam

Being Scared

When I was 6 I watched 'Scary Movie'
It's ghostly
I was forced by my big sister
But when I got to bed . . .
I heard *'Whoooo'*
Then something was crawling
Under the covers
Grabbed my legs
Then *arrgghh!*
I cried but then I
Was angry
Because
It was my big
Sister!

Natasha Vassell (9)
St Dunstan's CE Primary School, Cheam

Heebie-Jeebies

When I stay up late
I like to listen to heebie-jeebie stories
They get me all tingly inside
But when Mum sees me
I have to dash, cos Mum
Can give me a hefty great *slap!*

When I stay up late
I like to listen to heebie-jeebie stories
They give me an idea of adventure
I sail the seven seas until I fall
Asleep on the kitchen floor

When I stay up late
I like to listen to heebie-jeebie stories
They give me a feeling
But I have to slip back to my room
Cos my eyes are starting to close

When I stay up late
I like to listen to heebie-jeebie stories
They give me a strange feeling inside.

Lydia Blagden (8)
St Dunstan's CE Primary School, Cheam

Don't Call Piranha Big Belly Till You Cross The River
(Based on 'Don't Call Alligator Long-Mouth Till You Cross The River' by John Agard)

Call piranha big-belly
Call piranha small-tail
Call piranha red-teeth
Call piranha large-eyes
Call piranha tiny-mouth
Call piranha giant-head
Call piranha all them rude words
But better wait till you cross the river.

Verity Patmore (8)
St Dunstan's CE Primary School, Cheam

If You Want To See A Tiger

If you want to see a tiger
You must go to the dark, scary heart
Of the old doomed jungle

I know a tiger
Who's living down there -
He's mean, he's fierce, he's quick, he's roaring

Yes, if you really want to see a tiger
You must go to the dark, scary heart
Of the doomed jungle

Go down quietly and say
'Tiger come
Tiger come
Tiger coooommmme'

And he will leap out of the bushes
But don't stay for long
Run away!

Alexander Woolford (8)
St Dunstan's CE Primary School, Cheam

Don't Call A Horse Smelly-Mouth Till You Cross The Field

(Based on 'Don't Call Alligator Long-Mouth Till You Cross The River' by John Agard)

Call horse smelly-mouth
Call horse mad-eater
Call horse scissor-teeth
Call horse scrappity-rag
Call horse bite-eater
Call horse galloping-rag
Call horse fat-bum
Call horse all them rude words
But better wait
Till you cross the field.

Grace Hunter (9)
St Dunstan's CE Primary School, Cheam

Which Dog?

I said:
'I'd like a palace dog
A cricket player D Kallis dog
Or maybe even a cocky dog!'

Dad said:
'Oooh noo!
A chocky dog, a chucky dog
Wait! A hockey, stocky, shocky dog!'

At the pound it looked mucky
And there was a hound that smelt yucky!

Mum said:
'I'd like a poundy, houndy dog
A moundy, roundy dog
Then again it could be tizzy maybe frizzy!'

Keeper said:
'We've got Scotty dogs
Spotty dogs, trotty, potty, knotty dogs
You can have 'serve your tea' dogs
Or even 'win the lottery' dogs!'

Sister said:
'I want a cat dog, a rat dog
A silly little mat dog!'

Brother said:
'I want a hat dog, a bat dog
And to add to that . . .
A 'sit on your lap' dog!'

In the end we bought a D Kallis, hocky, poundy, houndy,
moundy, roundy, Scotty, 'serve your tea', 'win the lottery', 'sit on your lap' dog.

But it started bowling swingers at us
Hitting hockey pucks at us
And kept changing its face at us
Speaking Scottish to us
Not to mention smashing teacups at us!

Its way of winning the lottery was to buy a million tickets
We took it back and in the end we bought a cat!

Peter Buckley (10)
St Dunstan's CE Primary School, Cheam

Jeepers

The knock on the door scared me from sleep
As my aunt came in to watch the dreaded creep
I stayed up watching it, I didn't bear to peep
As the creeper pulled off his mask and scared me to sleep

I woke up in the night and saw a black thing
It was right in front of my nose and my eyes started to sting
They were stinging even more now so I started sleeping
In the morning I started thinking that jeeper was only
A
Thing!

Thomas Jeavons (9)
St Dunstan's CE Primary School, Cheam

Aiwwic, The Elf

A t 8.00 I overheard a scary story,
  I t was about a naughty elf
W ho knocked down walls, hills and houses.
W hen I went to bed
  I saw a shadow, small, pointy ears, spiky
  C laws . . . phew! It's only my Robin Hood teddy.

Joshua Higgs (8)
St Dunstan's CE Primary School, Cheam

Don't Call Parrot Sharp Picker Till You Cross The Rainforest
Based on 'Don't Call Alligator Long-Mouth Till You Cross The River' by John Agard)

Call parrot sharp-picker
Call parrot stripy-feather
Call parrot copy-cat
Call parrot rainbow-bum
Call parrot beady-eyes
Call parrot all them rude words
But better wait
Till you cross the rainforest.

Sian Kelly (9)
St Dunstan's CE Primary School, Cheam

Jack Horner

This is a rap
About little Jack Horner
He rose from his chair
In the little black corner
He liked his pie
He liked his plum
So he said to his mum
'Yum, yum, yum!'

Phoebe Dynan-Lewis (7)
St Dunstan's CE Primary School, Cheam

Colourful Butterfly

I'm a butterfly shining bright
In the gleaming morning light
When I spread my wings to fly
I circle across the morning sky
I search for my nectar in the flowers
In the early morning hours!

Tessa Caussyram (8)
St Dunstan's CE Primary School, Cheam

Friends

Friends are people that care for you
Always there and forever true
They make you laugh when you are down
To make a smile and stop the frown
At school they are a lot of fun
Whatever the weather, in the rain or sun
They make the school a happy place
With laughing eyes and a smiling face
They mean a lot, I care about them
And I would not like to be without them.

Emily Reynolds (8)
St Dunstan's CE Primary School, Cheam

A Naughty Elf

'It wasn't me,' I said
'Who got chocolate on my bed
I didn't make all that mess
I didn't lose my spelling test
I didn't make my sister cry
I didn't make her teddy fly
I didn't knock the glass off the shelf
I think it was a naughty elf.'

Edward Blythe (7)
St Dunstan's CE Primary School, Cheam

Nursery Rhyme Rap

This is a rap
About little Jack Horner
He started to live in a little dark corner
He liked his pie
He liked his plum
And after he had finished
He would say, 'Yum, yum!'

Stewart Reed (8)
St Dunstan's CE Primary School, Cheam

If You Want To See A Tiger

If you want to see a tiger
You must go down to the mad
Crazy end of the jungle

I know a tiger
Who's living down there
He's nasty, he's spoilt
He's fierce, he's huge

Yes, if you really want to see a tiger
You must go down to the mad
Crazy end of the jungle

Go down quietly and say
'Stupid tiger!
Stupid tiger!
Stupid tiiiiiiger!'

And he will creep out
But don't stick around
Run for your life!

Sophie Tonge (7)
St Dunstan's CE Primary School, Cheam

If I Had Wings

If I had wings
I would gaze at the earth
I would fly to the top of Mount Everest

If I had wings
I would taste the clouds
And fire small stars

If I had wings
I would sniff the fresh air
And I would swoop down to get my dinner.

Serena Shirley (7)
St Dunstan's CE Primary School, Cheam

If You Want To See A Tiger

If you want to see a tiger
You must go down to the creepy, crawly forest

I know a tiger
Who's living down there -
He's a creeper, he's a roarer, he's a mean tiger

Yes, if you really want to see a tiger,
You must go down to the creepy, crawly forest

Go down to the creepy, crawly forest and say
'Hello tiger
Hello tiger
Hello tiiiiiger'

And he'll jump up
And roar so much, don't stick around
Run for your life!

Victoria Goodridge (8)
St Dunstan's CE Primary School, Cheam

Sun

I love sun,
A hot day is fun,
Jump in the big pool,
Fizzy drinks keep you cool,
Play football at the park,
When there is a throw-in make sure you mark,
Summer is a good time,
Everybody is nice and fine,
Look at the big and flowery plants,
Make sure you don't get bitten by the red ants,
Oh, I just love the sun.

Jaime-Leane Lloves (7)
St Dunstan's CE Primary School, Cheam

Devils

Devils are red
Devils are dead
Devils are mean
Devils can't eat
Devils can't sleep
When you see
A devil dying
Punch him in the head
No devils are good.

Samuel Griffiths (8)
St Dunstan's CE Primary School, Cheam

The Magic Box

(Inspired by 'Magic Box' by Kit Wright)

I will put in my box
The sight of a swooping golden eagle
I will put in my box
The smell of a fire-breathing dragon
I will put in my box
The sound of a squawking parrot
I will put in my box
The taste of chocolate.

Samuel Nicholson (7)
St Dunstan's CE Primary School, Cheam

My Perfect Pet . . .

He always does my homework
He never needs a walk
He tidies up my bedroom
He always wants to talk.

Jake Worne (7)
St Dunstan's CE Primary School, Cheam

Summer

Summer has begun,
Me and my sister are playing in the sun,
We are all going to the beach,
With a bucket and a juicy peach,
I splash my brother in the salty sea,
I splash my brother and he splashed me,
Then we all go back home
And me and my brother start to moan,
We all go to bed
And I rest my head.

Martha Hamilton (7)
St Dunstan's CE Primary School, Cheam

I Love The Snow

I love the snow, it makes everything white
I like the way it sparkles at night

I like making snowballs, icy and cold
I throw them at Dad, I'm ever so bold

I love the snow, it's like cotton wool,
It's freezing, it's crunchy, it's crispy
It's cool!

Megan Baker (7)
St Dunstan's CE Primary School, Cheam

Dolphins

Dolphins are swimming in the sea
When I look at them they swim to me
And when I get in and hold their tails
They swim around me with the whales.

Lucy Alder (7)
St Dunstan's CE Primary School, Cheam

If You Want To See A Tiger

If you want to see a tiger
You must go down to the giant, scary
Heart of the jungle

I know a tiger
Who's living down there -
He's mean, he's scary, he's fierce
He's hairy

Yes, if you really want to see a tiger
You must go down to the giant, scary
Heart of the jungle

Go down to that jungle and say
'Tiger dada
Tiger dada
Tiger dadaaaaaa'

And out he will come
But don't stay and watch
Run for your life!

Alexander Tresadern (7)
St Dunstan's CE Primary School, Cheam

Jelly Can You Rap?

(Based on 'Gran Can You Rap' by Jack Ousbey)

'Jelly can you rap, can yer, can yer?'
'Oh yes I can, I'm a flip-flop, pip-pop, dip-dop
Drip-drop, rap, rap queen
I can whippy cream into a dream as I rap, rap, rap
I'm a chip-chap, dip-dap, flip-flap, bottle crack, rap, rap queen
See me wobble, see me wibble, see me wiggle around the pickle'
'Jelly can you rap, can yer?'
'Yes I can, I'm a raspberry ripple delicious tipple
Mouth-watering, mumbling, rumbling jelly!'

Kieran O'Toole (7)
St Dunstan's CE Primary School, Cheam

If You Want To See A Tiger

If you want to see a tiger
You must go down the long grass
In the middle of the jungle

I know a tiger
Who's living down there
He's mean, he's fierce, he's wicked
He's big

Yes, if you really want to see a tiger
You must go down the long grass
In the middle of the jungle

Go down slowly and say
'Tiger boy
Tiger boy
Tiger boyyyyy'

And he'll walk up slowly
But don't stick around
Run for your life!

Luke Aziz (8)
St Dunstan's CE Primary School, Cheam

In The Land Of The Giggly Boo!

In the land of the giggly boo
The people are red, white and blue
Their noses felt like their closes
As if they felt like you!

In the land of the giggly boo
It's a place for a giggly chat
With the cat with the white and black hat
Standing in the zoo

In the land of the giggly boo!

Olivia Taylor (8)
St Dunstan's CE Primary School, Cheam

If You Want To See A Tiger

If you want to see a tiger
You must go to the grassy, creepy Munga rainforest

I know a tiger who's living down there -
He's mean, he's sly, he's fierce, he's fast

Yes, if you really want to see a tiger
You must go to the grassy, creepy Munga rainforest

Go down quickly and say
'Tiger roar
Tiger roar
Tiger roarrrrrrr'

And he'll jump out of the bushes
But don't stick around
Run for your life!

Ryan Ford (8)
St Dunstan's CE Primary School, Cheam

Skiing For The First Time

I have just been skiing for the first time
It was fun to put all the heavy gear on
Waterproof clothes
Heavy ski boots on my feet
Headband to keep my ears warm
Helmet to protect my head
Gloves to keep my hands safe

I have just been skiing for the first time
On go my skies and up I go on the chairlift
Down I come shooting and whizzing
Stop!

Aaron Wade (8)
St Dunstan's CE Primary School, Cheam

Aliens Invaded Our House

One fine night
When I was asleep
I heard a slight creak
I went downstairs
And found an alien
Inspecting our pears

I let out a scream
And let out a cry
Then saw my brother, Guy
He let out a scream
And he saw the alien
With its teeth that gleam

Suddenly I recognised
It was a girl
With a beautiful, blonde curl.

Joshua Dawson (8)
St Dunstan's CE Primary School, Cheam

Lies

My friend lies a lot
She lies just for fun
My friend lies a lot
She lies for a hot cross bun

My friend lies a lot
She lies once or twice
My friend lies a lot
She lies for pet mice

My friend lies a lot
She lies all over the place
And where these lies come from
Is her dad's suitcase.

Alice Bailey (7)
St Dunstan's CE Primary School, Cheam

Bumblebee

My bumblebee flies
To each flower collecting nectar
As he goes along Mr Bumblebee
Buzzes a peaceful hum
As he goes along
I love my bumblebee
And he loves me so much!

Harriet Skinner (8)
St Dunstan's CE Primary School, Cheam

Out Of Space

On Monday morning as I walked to school,
I saw an alien from out of space in church hall,
Then it was time for the bell to ring,
Today a special person was coming to school called the king,
Again I saw the alien from out of space,
Somehow it was racing.

Alister Smith (8)
St Dunstan's CE Primary School, Cheam

If I Had Wings

If I had wings
I will fly up to the sky
And I will straighten my wings every day
If I had wings I would
Fly up and up.

Jade Holyoake (7)
St Dunstan's CE Primary School, Cheam

A Zegreb

The Zegreb is
Faster than snow drifting from the sky
Its has more body hair than a man's body
Its fang is longer than a crooked stick
Its brain is as small as a squashed pea
Its eyes are as red as hot fire
Its horns are stronger than an ox
Its head is hotter than lava.

James Buxton (8)
St Dunstan's CE Primary School, Cheam

My Kitten

My kitten is so puffy
She is very, very fluffy
She is the best in the world
I am never mad
I am never sad
She always comes to me.

Amelia Ford (7)
St Dunstan's CE Primary School, Cheam

Unfair

I climbed a tree
And hurt my knee
A bee came along
Singing a song
And decided to sting me!

Poppy Milton-Tomkins (7)
St Dunstan's CE Primary School, Cheam

My Mad And Bad Dog

Dad said, 'I want a small but tall dog, a cute one but a mute one'
I said, 'I want a mad and bad dog, a dumb one but a fun one'
Mum said, 'I want a cruel dog, I want a mean dog, but a 'sit on
your knee' dog'
Brother said, 'I want a big dog, one that digs and eats twigs'
Sister said, 'I want a flat dog who sits on the mat dog, who never gets
up and chews on a cup'
So I went into the pet shop and I saw this adorable
mad and bad, fun but dumb dog *and we got it!*

Jake Heasman (9)
St Dunstan's CE Primary School, Cheam

Autiviit Monster

At 10pm in the night I heard a noise,
It sounded like a soft gliding creature,
I didn't know what to do, so I crept out,
Then there was a black shape gliding in front of me,
With eyes on the back of its head,
I started to panic, my heart pumped furiously,
I ran into my room and jumped under the covers,
The cover was black, everything was black.

Nicholas Suchy (9)
St Dunstan's CE Primary School, Cheam

War

War is the colour of a dark, dark red
It smells like rotting flesh
It tastes like rotten salad mixed in raw fish
It sounds like people screaming with pain
War feels like pain, cruelty and dying
War lives everywhere, you can't destroy it, war is everywhere.

Kolujo Abraham (9)
St Dunstan's CE Primary School, Cheam

My Pet

I said to my mum and dad, 'I want a fish,' so we agreed.
I said, 'I want a flat fish, an old bumpy silly fish.'
Mum said, 'I want a soft fish, a funny old soft fish.'
Dad said, 'I want a *big* fish, a very, very *big* fish.'
My baby sister said, 'I want a floppy fish, a floppy, floppy fish.'
So we asked the shopkeeper,
The shopkeeper said, 'I would have a bony fish, that's the fish for me.'
In the end we all decided to get a multicoloured fish.
The colours were . . .
Green, yellow, pink, brown, orange, red, blue, black, white
Silver, gold and lots more.
We went home happily and loved our new fish!

Sarah Dalley (10)
St Dunstan's CE Primary School, Cheam

Guess Who?

I love to walk about at night in the gloomy streets
And wherever I go at night, who do I dare to meet
But mice, which is who I'd like to eat

And have you remembered what I said about being safe at night?
Well sorry, but I'm wrong because be sure to get a fright
So who do you think I am, telling you stuff like the word 'rat'?
Well, I am a mean, black c*at!*

Laura Cotzias (10)
St Dunstan's CE Primary School, Cheam

Dolphin

The silky soft skin of a wet dolphin
And the forward flip of a talented dolphin
The click and squeak of the little dolphins playing
And the silent noise of a dolphin catching her prey.

Lillie Garcia-Santos (7)
St Dunstan's CE Primary School, Cheam

If You Want To See A Tiger

If you want to see a tiger
You must go deep down into
The heart of the spooky forest.
I know a tiger
Who's living down there,
He's mean. He's sly. He's quick.
He's big.
Yes, if you really want to see a tiger,
You must go to the scary, dark, creepy forest
Where the tiger shall lie.
Go down to the forest and say,
'Tiger come
Tiger come
Tiger come!'

And out she will come
But don't hang about
Run for your life!

Nicholas Thomson (8)
St Dunstan's CE Primary School, Cheam

Trouble Going To The Zoo

One, two,
We're going to the zoo.
Mummy started to nag,
She lost her bag,
She found it in the sand.
My baby hit his hand,
He got mad,
Mum said he was bad.
Three, four
Open the door.
We're here at the gate,
I hope we're not too late.

Jeanie Gelling (8)
St Dunstan's CE Primary School, Cheam

I'm Sleeping!

When I try to get to sleep,
The children constantly keep
Dangling a mouse in front of me,
When I open my eyes that's all I can see.

They roll a ball across the floor,
When it finally hits the door,
The ball goes bang,
The bell inside goes clang.

I yet again wake up,
This time I've had enough,
Then I hiss,
But I make sure I miss.

Children can be very fun,
Some only have to put up with one!

Alice Graves (9)
St Dunstan's CE Primary School, Cheam

London

Phew! Stinky! In-your-face smell!
Rats are on the floor as well,
McDonald's! Pizza! Burger King!
There's something else to add to the din!

Yet Paris is a lovely city,
Oh so clean and ever so pretty!
But London is a horrid place,
With hardly any space.

When I am older I'll take a ride,
I'll go and live in the countryside.

Aimée Nott (9)
St Dunstan's CE Primary School, Cheam

Forgotten

In the towering shadows he lies,
Watching, waiting,
Staring out with saddened eyes,
Loathing, hating,
The family are in the kitchen,
Yelling, shouting,
He hears the upset children,
Crying, pouting,
A family row is taking place,
With screaming, slapping,
As he bounds through the door,
Biting, yapping,
Silence falls all around,
Quiet, stillness,
Guilt is in the air,
Cruelty, meanness,
With one last look,
He departs for evermore.

Georgina Bailey (9)
St Dunstan's CE Primary School, Cheam

The Superfanterpendous Thing

There's a superfanterpendous thing,
I know what it is,
It's lurking in your bath tub,
Waiting to be king.

It might be upon a shelf,
Or it's in a box,
It sometimes hunts for food,
It is a furry fox.

William Tsang (8)
St Dunstan's CE Primary School, Cheam

The Last Day

The last day at my school,
It's really not very cool,
To make new friends
And never let you borrow pens,
I'd rather stay here with my mates,
Instead of making boy/girlfriends and some dates,
I'll miss all the teachers,
I hope next year they won't be covered in leeches,
Goodbye my school and good luck,
Year 6 girls find a good school
And with your boyfriends don't get stood up.

Roseanne Minnette (9)
St Dunstan's CE Primary School, Cheam

Trees

Spring, summer, autumn and winter,
Each tree has a different colour,
Spring, they are growing,
Summer, they're green,
Autumn, they're brown,
Winter is clean,
Because trees are beautiful, so let them grow,
Especially in winter when they're covered in snow.

Kirsty Macphie (10)
St Dunstan's CE Primary School, Cheam

War

War is a deep dark red
It smells of blood and rotten flesh
War tastes of burning fire and broken wood
It sounds like catapults firing and swords clashing together
War feels like pain and death
War lives in the heart of a battlefield.

Joseph Murphy (9)
St Dunstan's CE Primary School, Cheam

Don't Call Tiger Curly Stripes Till You Cross The Jungle
(Based on 'Don't Call Alligator Long-Mouth Till You Cross The River' by John Agard)

Call tiger curly-stripes
Call tiger fat-stripes
Call tiger straight-stripes
Call tiger cloppy-stripes
Call tiger all those rude words
But better wait
Till you cross the jungle.

Katherine O'Reilly (9)
St Dunstan's CE Primary School, Cheam

Don't Call Bulldog Wimpy-Growl Till You Cross The Garden
(Based on 'Don't Call Alligator Long-Mouth Till You Cross The River' by John Agard)

Call bulldog wimpy-growl
Call bulldog smelly-growl
Call bulldog scaredy-growl
Call bulldog floppy-growl
Call bulldog ladybird-growl
Call bulldog all these rude words
But better wait
Till you cross the garden.

Samuel Higgs (8)
St Dunstan's CE Primary School, Cheam

Joy

Joy is the colour of the sky
Joy tastes like sweets
It smells as sweet as a candle
It feels so soft
Joy sounds like a bird singing
Joy lives on the Earth peacefully.

Brooklyn Gardner (10)
St Dunstan's CE Primary School, Cheam

Don't Call Stonefish No-Poison Till You Cross The Shallows
(Based on 'Don't Call Alligator Long-Mouth Till You Cross The River' by John Agard)

Call stonefish no-poison
Call stonefish easy-poison
Call stonefish pimpsy-poison
Call stonefish undeadly-poison
Call stonefish quiet-poison
Call stonefish all those rude words
But better wait
Till you cross the shallows.

Ethan Hall (9)
St Dunstan's CE Primary School, Cheam

Don't Call Tiger Long-Stripes Till You Cross The Jungle
(Based on 'Don't Call Alligator Long-Mouth Till You Cross The River' by John Agard)

Call tiger long-stripes
Call tiger black-stripes
Call tiger thin-stripes
Call tiger straight-stripes
Call tiger light-stripes
Call tiger all those rude words
But better wait
Till you cross the jungle.

Francesca Mongiovi (9)
St Dunstan's CE Primary School, Cheam

Peace

Peace is a dove floating in the air,
It smells like sweet perfume,
Peace tastes like a river of chocolate,
It feels soft and light,
Peace lives in Heaven.

Koyejo Abraham (9)
St Dunstan's CE Primary School, Cheam

Don't Call A Shark Puppy-Teeth
(Based on 'Don't Call Alligator Long-Mouth Till You Cross The River' by John Agard)

Call a shark puppy-teeth
Call a shark baby-teeth
Call a shark blunt-teeth
Call a shark ragged-teeth
Call a shark tiny-teeth
Call a shark wobbly-teeth
Call a shark silly-teeth
Call a shark funny-teeth
Till you cross the long dark sea.

Kristian Childs (9)
St Dunstan's CE Primary School, Cheam

Courage

Courage is yellow, to brighten up our lives,
Red for passion,
Black for strength,
It tastes like milk to make you strong,
It sounds like metal forging a perfect blade,
It feels like bravery in an outnumbered battle
Courage comes from the heart of God!

Robert Reed (9)
St Dunstan's CE Primary School, Cheam

My Family

F or everyone there's a family,
A dopted or not,
M y family is loving and caring,
I love them with all my heart and soul,
L ove is the most powerful thing in a family,
Y ours is special and so is mine!

Jessica Doyle (10)
St Dunstan's CE Primary School, Cheam

The Cake Shop

There's rock cakes,
Eccles cakes
And all kinds of speckled cakes.

There's wedding cakes,
Birthday cakes
And all kinds of special cakes.

There's fairy cakes,
Butterfly cakes
And all kinds of party cakes.

There's chocolate cakes,
Carrot cakes,
Oh what a hard decision to make.

Joshua Saliba-Graves (8)
St Dunstan's CE Primary School, Cheam

War

War is the colour of dark diseased blood.
War smells like moulding wood with slugs
(And mini-beasts) all over it.
War tastes like plain hate,
Moulding flesh with maggots,
Centipedes, millipedes and spiders.
War sounds like guns firing,
Swords clashing, horses clattering
And worst of all *death!*
War feels like the pain of a hundred houses on top of you.
War lives in *Hell!*

Michael Buckley (9)
St Dunstan's CE Primary School, Cheam

Mermaid And Chips

I went for a walk beside the water
And there I saw Neptune's daughter

Sitting up upon the rock
Where the seagulls usually flock

Dolphins diving in and out
Then in the distance came a shout

Neptune's calling for his girl
In his hand he clasped a pearl

Off she goes to swim with fish
Wouldn't she make a tasty dish!

With some chips and tartar sauce
And some mushy peas of course.

Abigail Saliba-Graves (10)
St Dunstan's CE Primary School, Cheam

I Would Like To Be By The Sea

I would like to be by the sea
With its soft yellow sand
And its rippling waves.

I would like to be by the sea
Making sandcastles
And swimming in the ocean.

I would like to be by the sea
Fishing far from shore,
Whilst swimming with the dolphins.

I would like to be by the sea.

Georgia Rivers (10)
St Dunstan's CE Primary School, Cheam

A Pond

A pond far away
That I go to see every day,
It's calm and refreshing
All the time,
That it clears my mind every time.

The pond has shoal of fishes
At all times
And they all come for feeding
At certain times.

Ducks and ducklings swim by
And sometimes it's hard to say goodbye,
The plants are soft and lovely all inside,
I wish I could be there somehow.

Yohannah Caussyram (9)
St Dunstan's CE Primary School, Cheam

My Dog, Fudge

My dog, Fudge
He sometimes holds a grudge
If we don't give him attention
He puts us in detention

My dog, Fudge
He often doesn't budge
He always lays around the place
But show him a squirrel and he's on the case

My dog, Fudge
He sits there like a judge
Very proud and very fluffy
I love him lots - although he's scruffy!

Alex Douglas (9)
St Dunstan's CE Primary School, Cheam

People

People run, people rush
People shove, people push
All they think about are pennies and pounds
Not the poor people that wait to be found
If one small thought could be spared for these
They could have food like fresh carrots and peas

Not all people are like this
They welcome the needy with a hug and a kiss

People should care, people should share
All these children, babies and more
Should not be turned away from your door
They need love that we can give
With our help a normal life they can live

As the end of my message grows near
Take care of those people who live in fear.

Alida Wotherspoon (10)
St Dunstan's CE Primary School, Cheam

War And Love

War
War is the colour of dark red
War smells like rotten bodies and blood
War tastes like a hot river that burns your tongue
War sounds like shields, swords and people shouting
War feels like sharp, rough and has pain
War lives in the heart of a battlefield

Love
Love is the colour of pink
Love smells like lavender and roses
Love tastes like milky chocolate
Love sounds like laughter and joy
Love feels smooth, fluffy and soft
Love lives in the heart of people.

Joseph Ahn (10)
St Dunstan's CE Primary School, Cheam

What Is Gold?
(Based on 'What Is Pink?' by Christina Rossetti)

What is gold? A crown is gold,
For a king that is very old.

What is blue? The sea is blue,
We can call it the ocean too.

What is red? Blood is red,
Sometimes it trickles into my bed.

What is blond? My hair is blond,
Unless I dunk it in a pond.

What is grey? Coins are grey,
So when I shop, I can pay.

What is black? A dog's nose is black,
Just like my dog, Mack.

What is green? Grass is green,
It is just a lovely scene.

What is orange? An orange is orange,
Why, just an orange.

Michael Crozier (8)
St Dunstan's CE Primary School, Cheam

I Asked A Blind Boy

I asked a blind boy what the colour blue was,
He said it was the colour of peace and hope,
I asked a blind boy what the colour of red was,
'Red is the colour of war, death and starvation,' he answered.
I asked a blind boy what the colour of yellow was,
The blind boy smiled and explained that yellow was the colour of happiness, the colour of smiles,
I asked a blind boy what the colour of pink was,
'Love,' he whispered, 'what the colour pink is, is love.'

Priya McQuaid (11)
St Dunstan's CE Primary School, Cheam

One Year

Spring
Spring is a warm welcome,
A time to open your mind,
Its new life brings new hope,
The sound of the birds returns

Summer
Summer is a holiday
A beautiful warm comfort
A relaxing movement
A happy day

Autumn
Autumn brings wind and rain
It blows over trees and leaves
It's a staying in season
A moment wanting to pass

Winter
Winter freezes the sun
Its snow brings fun and cold fingers
A time that's cold and wet
The snowman will guard its ice.

Savannah Worne (9)
St Dunstan's CE Primary School, Cheam

Spid The Spider

Spid the spider
Drank some cider
In his own swimming pool

He tried to swim
But couldn't float
Because he was a fool

As he sunk
He lost his trunks
Which wasn't very cool.

Alexander Blagden (8)
St Dunstan's CE Primary School, Cheam

Under The School

Under the school where everybody goes,
Is a little golden jacket for someone who knows.
Belongs to a brownie or maybe an elf
Like the one I saw upon my shelf.

Above the school where they can escape
To cover their eyes they wear a black cape,
But why do these awful and kind creatures
Spend all their time playing with the teachers?

Supanika Richmond (9)
St Dunstan's CE Primary School, Cheam

Youth

Youth is multicoloured,
Youth smells like fun,
Youth tastes like chocolates and sweets,
Youth sounds like music,
Youth feels soft and jumpy,
Youth lives in the heart of people.

Amy Swansbury (10)
St Dunstan's CE Primary School, Cheam

Morning Rises

As the morning rises by the ticking clock
Silly mice eat a dumped cardboard box
When the horses neigh in their stables
A baby cries in its cradle

As maids clean wooden floors
A beggar boy sits there bored
All by the morning rises.

Omar Rana (9)
St Dunstan's CE Primary School, Cheam

Cheam Park

Through Cheam Park I walk each day,
Gravel path this is the way,
I travel along its route to school,
Or maybe scooting, it's just cool!
Puffy clouds, bleached so white,
Dewy grass, shines so bright.

The enchanted wood, beautiful trees,
Holey bumps like knobbly knees!
Wind whistling, dogs barking,
Robins chirping, children laughing.
End of the path, out we crawl,
And across the road, then go to school.

Afternoon, trundling back,
Book bags and trainers, make the pack.
Summer park, the sun is hot,
Take my coat? I think not!
Bucket and spade for the sand,
And dig a hole with my hand.

Evening breeze, time to go,
Squirrels skip in bushes down low.
Right up high in the trees,
Blackbirds disturb rustling leaves.
Into the car, turn the key,
Cheam Park is a wonder to see!

Samuel Berry (9)
St Dunstan's CE Primary School, Cheam

Love

Love is red like roses
Love smells like flowers
Love tastes like food
Love sounds like laughter
Love feels like you can fly
Love lives in the heart.

Benjamin Cummings-Montero (9)
St Dunstan's CE Primary School, Cheam

The Chinese Dragon

The Chinese dragon
Waving its purple hair,
The Chinese dragon
The cymbals clash through the air.

The drummers beat the drums,
The gong players chime the gongs,
The echo of the claves ring in the air,
Causing people to stop, stand and stare.

The Chinese dragon,
Its mean red eyes,
As bright as cosmic fire,
Sweeping through the air.

The Chinese dragon,
Twisting its snake-like body,
The Chinese dragon
Gone for another year.

Katy Pitcher (10)
St Dunstan's CE Primary School, Cheam

The Seaside

The sea is tough
The rocks are rough
The seaweed is slimy and green

Fish you will see
In the blue sea
Swimming through the waves

Ice creams you will eat
With sand on your feet
Walking on the sand dunes

It is sunny
My friend is funny
When I talk to her.

Charlotte Reynolds (9)
St Dunstan's CE Primary School, Cheam

Dragonball

Death Destruction KO you're out
Dragonball Z fighters are about

They're getting into action and they're ready to fight
Get out of their way or you won't live till tonight

Gohan, Trunks, Tien and Picalo
Napa, Cell, Krillen and Vageato

All battling it out who's gonna lose
It's your chance to bet so you better choose

Bibady, Bobady and out comes Boo
You better run, you better hide, they're coming for you

Destructo Disc, Wolf Fang Fist what will they choose?
Final flash buster canon Masinco blast don't matter you're gonna lose

Chichi flips out and goes into her mental mood
Too late Trunks and Gotan are already fused

They fly through the air planning each move
They have to be exact, they don't want to lose

Napa hits Goku with bomber DX
The crowd all watches, what's gonna happen next?

Tien's up next with his solar flare
Krillen goes down like a bird shot from the air

Picalo's beam cannon fires at Cell
It hits him in the stomach and he falls with a yell

As he hits the floor Radizt is there too
There are just a few left, what are they gonna do

Gohan is back with Kumykumyha
All are out except Yamcha

The fight's nearly over or that's what it seemed
But Freezer was back with his lethal death beam

The final blast made them all fall
Gohan stood, he had won the brawl.

Joshua Collyer (11)
St Dunstan's CE Primary School, Cheam

Scared!

I went through the day, I went through the night,
A whisper from the left, a whisper from the right,
M any people say, 'Follow your nose.'
S o I do it all the time, like a petal from a rose,
C an you hear that sound? It's coming from the ground,
A rattle and a shake, further than that lake.
R ummage through mud, looking for that thud,
E verything I see is not blind to you and me,
D on't just stand around, pull me out of the ground.

Jaya McQuaid (8)
St Dunstan's CE Primary School, Cheam

Don't Call Tiger Stupid-Stripes Till You Cross The Jungle

(Based on 'Don't Call Alligator Long-Mouth Till You Cross The River' by John Agard)

Call tiger stupid-stripes,
Call tiger silly-stripes,
Call tiger wobbly-stripes,
Call tiger fat-stripes,
Call tiger thin-stripes,
Call tiger all those rude words
But better wait
Till you cross the jungle!

Euan McGraw (8)
St Dunstan's CE Primary School, Cheam

Sounds

The loud pop of the fat balloon,
The soft creak of the huge door,
The loud sizzle of the fat sausages,
As they lay in the pan.

Katy Munson (7)
St Dunstan's RC Primary School, Woking

Christmas Colours

Red is the fire's flickering flames,
A stocking full of presents,
Silver could be sparkling halos
Or tinsel on the prickly Christmas tree,
White is snow fallen on the glittering ground,
Dresses of angels fluttering around,
Gold might be lights on a pointed Christmas tree
Or baubles dangling down from it,
Yellow is the waving of the candlestick,
Stars in the night sky.

Rosaleen Newell (8)
St Dunstan's RC Primary School, Woking

Touch

I like snowball fights
Hard and light
I like fireworks
Loud and quiet
I like feeling hot baths and shoulders
Sprinkling down my face
I like touching cold, icy snow
I like jumping in my clothes when they are washed
I like fluffy pillows when I go to bed.

Shannon Southey (7)
St Dunstan's RC Primary School, Woking

Untitled

I like the relaxing hot steam coming out of the bath
The smoothness of the wooden slippery floor
I like to feel the snow splatting on my face
I like the new fresh shirts out of the cupboard.

Daniel Cranstone (7)
St Dunstan's RC Primary School, Woking

Noises Everywhere!

Splash! The diver hit the water,
Quick, the swimmer piercing through the water,
The bubbles of the person
Like a bullet through the water.

The pop of the popcorn,
The crunches of the chocolate,
The slurp of the gobstopper
As it's stopping your mouth chatting to friends.

Georgia Taylor (7)
St Dunstan's RC Primary School, Woking

Sounds

The bang of the drum,
The squeak of the violin,
The ring of the doorbell,
The slam of the conker falling from the oak tree,
A creak of the door,
A thump of a punch,
A hiss of a snake,
A sniff of a dog,
A chirp of a bird.

James Kear (7)
St Dunstan's RC Primary School, Woking

Touch

I like the softness of my cat's fur
Smoothness of my walls in the kitchen
I like to feel the soft snow falling on my head
I like to feel the smooth wooden floor on my bare feet
I like my dad's hairy beard.

Olivia Ash (7)
St Dunstan's RC Primary School, Woking

Once Upon A Rhyme

Now it is spring,
There's lots of flowers,
All in a ring
And some in towers.

The lambs are dancing
Around and around,
The foals are prancing
And stamping on the ground.

Little paws pattering,
Along the floor,
With everyone chattering,
You can't wait for more!

The days are getting longer,
The leaves are getting green.
How long will this last?
It remains to be seen.

Megan Turner (9)
St Dunstan's RC Primary School, Woking

Sounds

The loud crash of the big glass,
The enormous blast of the doors,
The bang of the clock
As it goes tick-tock.

The roar of the bear,
The sniffing nose of the dog,
The purring of the cat
As it plays all the time.

The buzz of the honeybee,
The hum of the ladybird,
The woo of the owl
As it is in the tree.

Niamh Pinfield (7)
St Dunstan's RC Primary School, Woking

My Magic Box

(Based on 'Magic Box' by Kit Wright)

I will put into my box . . .

The first word of a baby
The last snowflake off a mountain
The first sting of a bee

I will put into my box . . .

The torn treasure map of a pirate
A trickle of water
The cackle of a witch

I will put into my box . . .

The feeling of Christmas coming
The sound of a newborn whale
The cry of joy on top of the Alps

My box is fashioned from . . .

The stars twinkling up from the sky
A spark from a fairy fire
The silky red ribbon around the edges

In my box I will

Swim with the soft, smooth dolphins
In the electric-blue, deep sea.

Natasha Dean (10)
St Dunstan's RC Primary School, Woking

Scary Night

The loud groaning of the rumbling radiator
The loud swishing of the three-headed ghost
The snoring and sleeping of the fire-tongued dragon
The dripping of the tap through the night
The howling of the werewolf in the moonlight.

Conor Edwards (7)
St Dunstan's RC Primary School, Woking

My Magic Box
(Based on 'Magic Box' by Kit Wright)

I will put into my box . . .

The first roar of a lion
The last jump of a dolphin
The first giggle of a baby

I will put into my box . . .

Some hairs of a kitten
A tusk of an elephant
A scale of a fish

I will put into my box . . .

The first hiss of a snake
The first bark of a dog
The first sound of a baby

My box is fashioned from the bluest part of the Atlantic
Gems waiting to keep a secret
Tears of joy down the sides

I shall explore the world and do everything with animals.

Jessica O'Callaghan (10)
St Dunstan's RC Primary School, Woking

Sounds

The smack of the football,
The splash of the swimmer,
The thud of the bat as the ball goes far.

The zooming of the F1,
The skidding of the motorbike
As he zooms through the finish line.

The thud of the basketball,
The smack of the snooker cue,
The swish of the surfer
As he zooms through the wave.

Nathan Ghouri (7)
St Dunstan's RC Primary School, Woking

The Magic Box
(Based on 'Magic Box' by Kit Wright)

I will put into my box . . .

A smile of a delighted friend
The splash of a tremendous dive
Cheers and hoorays from a succeeded crowd

I will put into my box . . .

The sand of a desert island
A wave of a surfing bay
Coral from a fascinating rock pool

I will put into my box . . .

The screams from a twisting roller coaster
Laughs from a funny ride
Looks of amazement from a human animal show

I will put into my box . . .

The silence of a reading child
Chuckle and laughter of playing children
The roars of triumph from a football team

My box is fashioned from shiny dust, water and paper
Unopened secrets at the bottom
With horse hair hinges

I shall ride on it as if it was a giraffe
Through the exciting jungle
Exploring and seeing a zoo of animals
Then I will come home.

Lily Rose Smith (9)
St Dunstan's RC Primary School, Woking

The Magic Box
(Based on 'Magic Box' by Kit Wright)

I will put into my box . . .

My family secrets of every cloudy clear Christmas I've shared
A kiss on a cheek from the fairest river
The deepest, darkest dream of a dragon

I will put into my box . . .

A pearl from the midnight misted moon
The last baa from a lamb of spring
The first glimpse of the future's setting secrets

I will put into my box . . .

The last snowflake of the season
The last cry of a baby
The last call of a cat

My box is fashioned from . . .
The first fairest sip of water
The feathers of a greatest eagle
The poshest pearls patterned from a kiss of welcome

I shall dance in the deepest, darkest, densest river
Declared on the densest days.

Lucy Fidge (10)
St Dunstan's RC Primary School, Woking

Colours Of Christmas

Gold is the blazing moon while the stars dance around her.

Silver is the frozen cold snow, when the snow breaks it turns into a puddle of frozen water, as blue and silver snowflakes tumble from the blue sky.

Purple is the fun colour for the Christmas tree's baubles.

Black is the frozen night in December
or as a piece of coal runs away from evil.

Sophie Federico (7)
St Dunstan's RC Primary School, Woking

The Magic Box
(Based on 'Magic Box' by Kit Wright)

I will put into the box . . .

The sound of a tinkling bell
The brightest star at night
The first cry of a newborn baby

I will put into the box . . .

Some perfect paintings, pretty and neat
A beam of bright sun
The first word of a toddler

I will put into the box . . .

A roar of a great lion
The memory of a great aunt
Great hills high in power

My box is fashioned from
The softest silk
The outside is wooden, deep pine
With a few pearls and cushions

I shall go in my box
To faraway lands
To go far and wide
Seeing and exploring
And having fun.

Charlotte Heffernan (10)
St Dunstan's RC Primary School, Woking

Sounds

The squeal and the squeaking of a little rat
Frozen in bed, nervous and panicking
A skeleton and a ghost, groaned and moaned
A pussy cat miaows and walks elegantly
Sensitive tail, miaow, miaow, how can she stop!

Helen Fenning (7)
St Dunstan's RC Primary School, Woking

The Magic Box
(Based on 'Magic Box' by Kit Wright)

I will put into the box . . .

The first tooth a baby grows,
A Bible that Jesus has blessed,
The first time I see my mum and dad.

I will put into the box . . .

The first friend I ever had
My first ever Christmas present
The first time I see my brother

I will put into the box . . .

A picture of me floating in mid-air
My first ever pet
A roar of a tamed lion

My box is fashioned from
Gold, silver and ice
From the Atlantic ocean

My secret's safe in the corner
Ready to pop out
When I open it.

Daniela Frangiamore (9)
St Dunstan's RC Primary School, Woking

I Am A Snowman

I am a snowman big and fat
I am a snowman with a hat
I'm so big and I'm so tall
Did I mention my name's Paul
The cat destroyed me
Now I'm small
Now they call me Snowball.

Felix Reilly (8)
St Dunstan's RC Primary School, Woking

The Magic Box
(Based on 'Magic Box' by Kit Wright)

I will put into my box . . .

The kick into goal that saves our team,
Someone to say to me, 'Brill, you're great!'
And the sensation of holding the golden cup.

I will put into my box . . .

The laughter of my dad
And the wonderful meals my mum cooks
And the first word I said.

I will put into my box . . .

My best friend Daniela
And the feeling of laughter
And the smell of Christmas dinner.

My box is made from diamonds
And seashells from the sea
And glistening gold hinges.

I shall
Swim with otters
And stroke their brown backs
And watch them eat crab and fish.

Elizabeth Fitzgerald (9)
St Dunstan's RC Primary School, Woking

Bubbles

Bubbles are fun
Bubbles are great
Bubbles are everywhere
Bubbles jump up and down
In the sky and say hello.

Zara Mizen (8)
St Dunstan's RC Primary School, Woking

Phoenix

I live a peaceful life in the sun really,
I wander day by day from star to sunny star,
I feed and die into ashes which feed the sun incredibly,
Then I am reborn as a baby, my golden wings flap as I feed
For the first time and then I blow the black, dead, lifeless
And fireless star to rest,
I have no real home, I just fly from star to sunny star.

Every so often I come upon an inhabited planet in the stars,
Every so often they see me and sometimes they don't,
Some planets such as Earth, the people believe it's an eclipse,
When I fly on my millennium journey around the galaxy.

More or less once a millennium I fly past Earth's star of gold,
My golden back is not what they see,
But the black fire on my underbelly is their sight,
My sight blocks their sun for no more than just a few seconds,
Can you guess who I am?

Nicholas Blackett (10)
St Dunstan's RC Primary School, Woking

Colours Of Christmas

Red is the colour of Father Christmas' sleigh
flying in the night sky.

White is the snow floating in the sky.

Green is the Christmas tree blowing to and fro
in the wind.

Silver is the ice melting on the car top.

Gold is the decoration on the Christmas tree
dangling down.

Yellow is the star over Jesus' head.

Blue is the bauble hanging on the tree.

Megan Hewson (7)
St Dunstan's RC Primary School, Woking

Blue

The waves roared and the sea whispered,
Leaving its blue breath on the shore,
Then the waves stopped as if a pair of hands had grasped the sea,
Leaving behind only sand on the shore.

Roar, roar, went the waves,
Whisper, whisper, went the sea,
The noise began to build up again,
Waves began dancing on the sea,
The sea playing slow music.

Silence struck,
All of a sudden the sea kept going out and in,
Like a skirt moving freely in the breeze,
Then the tide went out,
Leaving only seaweed and sand on the shore.

I rest my feet on the warm grains of sand
And watch the sun go down,
Then I walk back
And can still hear the waves roar.

Dominique Black (11)
St Dunstan's RC Primary School, Woking

You Are What You Eat

You are what you eat
From your head to your feet
They can see but nobody knows
You may have eaten an apple or pear
But now they've turned into your clothes.
You're covered in peel
From your head to your heel
You have no reason to wash
But you'd better watch out for human feet
Or you're going to end up squashed!

Siobhan Straver (8)
St Dunstan's RC Primary School, Woking

The Magic Box
(Based on 'Magic Box' by Kit Wright)

I will put in the box . . .

Three gold bars from ancient Egypt
An aeroplane to fly around the world in
A photo album to remind me of old times

I will put into the box . . .
A rocket car to see the sights of England
A planet that will be mine and only mine
A mansion to live and sleep in

I will put into the box . . .

A playground so I can play with my friend
A goat to sail the seas
A takeaway place at the end of my garden

I will put into the box . . .

A flying motorbike that speeds on water
A servant that will do whatever I want
Every single make of car in the world

It's made of shining silver
Glittering gold, soundproof windows
And heavily guarded by guns.

Matthew Kear (10)
St Dunstan's RC Primary School, Woking

Green

Green is slime and the colour of lime
Green is the colour of Henry's eyes
Green is the colour of grass
Green is the colour of jealousy
Green is the colour of leaves high up in the trees
Green is the colour of conker shells
Green is the colour we can't live without!

Robert Derienzo (7)
St Dunstan's RC Primary School, Woking

The Magic Box
(Based on 'Magic Box' by Kit Wright)

I will put into the box . . .

The carcass of a massive frog
The wisp of hot blue smoke and
The laugh of a lost child when it finds its mother

I will put into the box . . .

Good luck for me
A stretched limo to carry me away from my troubles
And an everlasting friend to play with

I will put into the box . . .

Burger King's best food
A football pitch to play on
And the first blink of a baby

My box is made of touchable fire
And a padlock on it too
Because of the rummaging secrets inside
And to keep my dreams and wishes safe

I will win football and all sports I've put in my box
And keep my box and its contents secret
Stored away in a secret stash in a secret safe.

Tom McPhee (9)
St Dunstan's RC Primary School, Woking

The Waterfall

Its long legs are jumping up and down,
It is spitting, while it swallows the ground,
It is yelling, come here, come here,
It's splashing,
Hitting the cliff it pounces and starts crying,
Then it lies there, dying.

Vince Russo (10)
St Dunstan's RC Primary School, Woking

The Magic Box
(Based on 'Magic Box' by Kit Wright)

I will put in my box . . .

A cuddle of cosy covers,
A deep, dark stream,
A warm, welcoming kiss.

I will put in my box . . .

The glimpse of the bright sun,
A flake of a snowman's belly,
A white daisy petal that never dies.

I will put in my box . . .

A motorbike on four wheels,
A car on two wheels, in my command,
A singing solo in the cosy countryside.

My box is fashioned from . . .

Shells from the seaside,
A sparkle of light blue sea,
In every corner gold wishes are granted.

I shall dance in my box
In the winter's wildness,
Land on a bright summer's day,
The dance shall never ever end.

Hannah Spruzs (10)
St Dunstan's RC Primary School, Woking

The Magic Box
(Based on 'Magic Box' by Kit Wright)

I will put into the box . . .

The last laugh from an old man
The first step from a baby
A bark from a guard dog

I will put into the box . . .

A golden everlasting sunset
A smile from a jumping dolphin
A feather from a talking bird

I will put into the box . . .

Three wishes from a whistling wizard
Melting lava from a hot volcano
And a gold coin

My box is made from
Gold and tin and silver
The hinges are made from frogs' legs
And it has flowers on the lid

I shall swim with dolphins
In the highest ocean of them all
And end up on a beach with
A huge yellow sun.

Anna Valentino (10)
St Dunstan's RC Primary School, Woking

The Magic Box
(Based on 'Magic Box' by Kit Wright)

I will put in my box . . .

All my memories of the past
The final laughs from my grandad
The first word from a baby

I will put in my box . . .

My secrets that have never been opened
Three wishes in code
The hair from my black and white cats

I will put in my box . . .

The sound of squealing, sacred dolphins
The sound of friends giggling
The sound of chatter in the classroom

My box is fashioned from
Love, all around it
Stars in every corner
With flowers on the lid

I shall snorkel with dolphins
In the Atlantic Ocean
And wash ashore on the Tenerife beach.

Amy Hull (10)
St Dunstan's RC Primary School, Woking

Topsy-Turvy

I like the softness of my silky duvet quilt,
The roughness of my bedroom floor,
I like the cold, icy snowflakes dropping from the sky.

Luke Middleton (8)
St Dunstan's RC Primary School, Woking

The Magic Box
(Based on 'Magic Box' by Kit Wright)

I will put in the box . . .

A breath of fire from the last dragon to live on Earth,
A sports car with 12 engines
And a golden note from my grandad.

I will put in my box . . .

The first breath of air that I took,
The speed of a speedboat,
The sunbeam that lights up the world.

I will put in my box . . .

An alive shark with loads of teeth,
A cute cat purring
And my mum and dad kissing me.

My box will have 2 locks opened by magic
And the outside will be made from feathers
Also the inside is very quiet
So I go to bed inside.

David Pinfield (10)
St Dunstan's RC Primary School, Woking

Snow-Capped Mountains

The snow-capped mountains sparkle all day
Shining, glistening they never do stop
The wondrous hills never go away
Clouds argue all the time, but they're never in a strop.

The mountains are so wonderful
Cool ice and snow cap their heads
Of course they are never dull
They'll always be there even when we're in our beds.

Francesca Brown (10)
St Dunstan's RC Primary School, Woking

What To Wear

It's the disco!
I don't know what to wear
Something fashionable
Anything spare?

I need something to eat
Maybe a pear
I'll have a sweet
Then I can share

I might wear a crop top
But I'd have to make sure
I don't drink any pop

I could wear some jeans
But then for my tea
I couldn't have beans

So what shall I wear?
Do you have anything spare?

Emily Woods (8)
St Dunstan's RC Primary School, Woking

Eve Of Christmas

The night is dark,
Its darkest ever,
The wind howls and cries as it swirls around,
Eagles fly out from the night,
Trees cower and huddle,
The moon watches over the city,
Leaves scuttle around,
Snow creates a blanket of white,
People throw snowballs,
Cars stop at the amazing power of Christmas.

Philip Moloney (10)
St Dunstan's RC Primary School, Woking

Giant Man

Iron Man, Iron Man
Tall as a giant man
Iron Man, Iron Man
Clank, clank, clank

Iron Man, Iron Man
Nuts, bolts, screws
Iron Man, Iron Man
Clank, clank, clank

Iron Man, Iron Man
Green eyes shining bright
Iron Man, Iron Man
Seeing through the night
Iron Man, Iron Man
Clank,
Clank,
Clank.

Antonio Procida (9)
St Dunstan's RC Primary School, Woking

My School

Have you ever been to my school?
It has a really big hall
And have you ever been in the swimming pool?
It is really nice and cool
And have you ever had school lunch?
You'll really like the punch
Have you ever done some art?
I drew a really nice go-kart
And have you ever been out to play?
You'll have a really nice day
My school is the best
But I really need to have a rest.

Lucia Caruso (9)
St Dunstan's RC Primary School, Woking

Cat

Cat
Naughty cat
Naughty cat running

Fox
Orange fox
Orange fox creeping

Tortoise
Slow tortoise
Slow tiptoeing tortoise

Elephant
Heavy elephant
Heavy elephant stomping

Pig
Pink pig
Pink pig smelling

Octopus
Scary octopus
Scary octopus wiggling.

Eleanor Knecht (7)
St Dunstan's RC Primary School, Woking

Day And Night

Sparkling in the night,
Twinkling stars shine bright.
Shining like a silver spoon
Is the light of the moon.

The sun rises in the morning,
Opening its eyes and yawning.
Another day starts,
As the night passes by.

Zara John (11)
St Dunstan's RC Primary School, Woking

Monkey

Monkey
Sly monkey
Sly monkey dancing

Cat
Cool cat
Cool cat purring

Bull
Strong bull
Strong bull roaring

Elephant
Naughty elephant
Naughty elephant giggling.

Lucinda Piazza (7)
St Dunstan's RC Primary School, Woking

Three In A Bed

Rabbit
Funny rabbit
Funny rabbit munching

Fish
Wet fish
Wet fish swimming

Hamster
Grey hamster
Grey hamster sleeping

Cat
Fluffy cat
Fluffy cat crunching.

Nadia Procida (8)
St Dunstan's RC Primary School, Woking

The Leaves' Playtime

Green, green leaves
On the brown trees
Watch them as I go
I'm off far away
From England
Off to New Zealand
Back in the garden
Leaves say pardon
Jump off trees
Go to the leaves
First play tag
In my bag
Then they eat
With the sleet
I come back
With a pack
You have been playing leaves
On those trees.

William Grigsby (8)
St Dunstan's RC Primary School, Woking

Four In A Bed

Monkey
Funny monkey
Funny monkey swinging

Dog
Barking dog
Barking dog playing

Fox
Scary fox
Scary fox sniffing

Tiger
Fierce tiger
Fierce tiger roaring.

Daniel Mulvihill (7)
St Dunstan's RC Primary School, Woking

Sounds

The buzz of the bumblebee,
The swish of the whale,
The roar of the lion,
The snap of the crocodile,
The squeak of the bird,
As they move everywhere.

The bark of the dog,
The moo of the cow,
The miaow of the cat,
The squeal of the mouse,
The snore of the pig,
As they move about.

The smash of the football,
The clash of the rugby ball,
The bang of the golf ball,
The boom of the cricket ball,
The smack of the tennis ball,
As the ball moves about.

Connor Moore (7)
St Dunstan's RC Primary School, Woking

Football Mad

I'm football mad
But I'm pretty bad
I can kick a ball into space
But then it'll land on my face

I'm football crazy
But I'm so lazy
I don't know what to do
Maybe I should ask you

I know, I'll go on a team
And I will just sheen
Oh but I'm bad
I'm just football *mad!*

Daniella Flint (11)
St Dunstan's RC Primary School, Woking

Snake

Snake
Sly snake
Sly snake fighting

Monkey
Brown monkey
Brown monkey dancing

Warthog
Fat warthog
Fat warthog munching

Lion
Strong lion
Strong lion roaring

Fish
Silly fish
Silly fish squirming

Wolf
Nasty wolf
Nasty wolf hunting.

Jack O'Callaghan (8)
St Dunstan's RC Primary School, Woking

Three In A Bed

Bull
Strong bull
Strong bull eating

T-rex
Fierce T-rex
Fierce T-rex hunting

Cheetah
Fast cheetah
Fast cheetah killing.

Cameron Grennan (8)
St Dunstan's RC Primary School, Woking

Crocodile Monster

The crocodile walks at night,
While the hunters try and catch
The sleeping monster at night.

It walks under a full moon,
To catch another victim nearby,
In the town of Lost Souls.
It never runs away
To another town for food
Because the town of Lost Souls is the scariest town ever,
Ghosts and ghouls hovering about,
Scare the people at night,
While they distract,
The monster takes its prey,
Every night . . .

Oliver Jordan (10)
St Dunstan's RC Primary School, Woking

The Wonders Of The Moon

As I watch every night,
She glows and lights the dark
And when I smile,
She twinkles back,
That wonderful sparkling light.

The luminous shimmer,
Reflected,
Reflected from the pond,
Her beauty and twinkle gleams,
As it stares me in the face.

The brilliant moon shines,
She shines all night
And best of all,
She is my light.

Cliona Moore (11)
St Dunstan's RC Primary School, Woking

Sea

She shines in the glistening sun
And sparkles like a diamond
Pirates racing in speedboats
For the hidden treasure
Beneath the ocean sands

Babies enjoying the rock pool
And parents taking a dip
Children soaking in
The ocean air
While archaeologists discover
More of the sea life

Waves jumping up and down
At the birds having
A fishy meal
And the shark looks for his

The sun spreads its golden rays
Across the diamond-covered sea
Then gazes at
The diamond-studded stars
And they twinkle back

The rim of the sea spinning
As free as a bird
And us fish swim away from
The huge nets that capture us.

Benhilda Mombo (10)
St Dunstan's RC Primary School, Woking

Love

L ove is a symbol of two hearts, perfect for each other
O n the second month of the year you shall reveal true love
V alentine's, when people share their true love for one another
E ndless love shall go on and on forever.

Carmina Gonzalez Gomez (11)
St Dunstan's RC Primary School, Woking

Imagination

In a ditch by a pitch,
Lies a marvellous thing
It sings ting-tong and bling-ching

Step inside
Be taken by the tide
Of imagination
Meet a creature
Not a preacher
Who loves personification

If you were to come across
A bit of moss
That has her own mind
Or a thread of grass who hasn't seen another of his kind!
How about a conifer, did you know he's blind?

You may meet an ogabooga
Or a noogagroka with a broken whistle
Saying that they are as tired as a lark
Or as thick as a thistle!

Would you give a kiss goodnight
To a boogadi-bite?
This little thing gives out a great height of fright!

Kind-hearted enough to sing a song so sweet
To an ezda with smelly feet?
No, of course not, it would stop your heartbeat!

Would you care for tiddly-tum because she doesn't have a mum?
But no, she may not have a mum but
She certainly has a big tum-tum

You'd better start getting back, it's 84 o'clock
Try and find the way to the imagination dock!
You'll be pushed out by the tide, please visit again -

You're back in the ditch by the pitch, you'd better run!

Roisin Straver (11)
St Dunstan's RC Primary School, Woking

Summer Sunset

The water colour waving goodbye
It welcomes the moon into the sky

A smiling face under balloons
The night is here very soon

The time for fairies to get to sleep
In their flowers neat and sweet

Peaceful at once
As the petals fade in their bunch

A lovely light
Before the night

The sun is about to hide
Where the moon is about to bite

The sun walks down from the sky
As the moon jumps up high!

Georgina Watkins (10)
St Dunstan's RC Primary School, Woking

Freaky Corridor

The bright red carpet and yellow wall
Even enough horror to make a cat squall
17 doors and so many places
200 huge mammals with such scary faces
Because the corridor is where all ants die
Big feet step on us and loved ones cry.

Because the corridor was once no-man's-land
The ants could have a party and create a band
But then the humans came and took over the floor
And now the corridor
        Is no more!

Paul Raleigh (11)
St Dunstan's RC Primary School, Woking

Evil Life

This is a strange life
Where dreams are feared
Where bugs leap
When monsters sleep
Where life does not matter

This is a good life
Where dragons fight
Like bees at night
No people are right
For the dead do not bite
Where life does of course matter

This is a long life
With fires and light
With frozen nights
Where life so long can matter

This is a dead life
Where genies rise
Like eagles on the marshlands
Where golden flies have smart bow ties
Where life is a powerful creature

This is a mad life
Where ogres glare
And wizards jump on brooms and fly
And diamond-encrusted birds
Crow and cry
When the monsters from the deep
Where life is silent but what is it . . .
Howling wolves or jumping fish
Or giant rocks or broken ships?
This life is so evil
Like a box of grief.

Edward Wilson (10)
St Dunstan's RC Primary School, Woking

The Magical Feather

Long, long ago,
In a land called Habberworth,
Where no one dared to go,
Lived a witch, with a feather.

Not just an ordinary feather,
A magical feather,
With its pearly white skin,
It will grant any wish,
You want or need.

See the future,
If you want,
Invisibility,
If you wish,
All you need to do
Is touch the feather
With a finger or two.

'Yes,' said Peter when he saw it,
'Another feather for my collection,
I shall pick it up
And . . .

Where am I? What is this feather?
Wow, a . . . a . . . magical feather,
It's mine,
It's mine,
I found it,
It's mine,' Peter sang with joy.

'Where is it? That special feather?' the witch exclaims,
'Darn, I've lost it!'

Olivia Frayne (11)
St Dunstan's RC Primary School, Woking

TV

The TV is a lifetime
It really wasn't Einstein

Hook it up to your PS2
What a brilliant thing to do

The TV is insane
ITV and 'You've Been Framed'

The TV is so cool
It really is a handy tool

At school you do division
At home it's television

EastEnders, Corrie and Emmerdale
Make you laugh and even wail

Soaps, films and quiz shows
Celebrities come to blows

Watching videos and DVDs
Eating chips and mushy peas

'I'm A Celebrity Get Me Out Of Here!'
Give the winner a great big cheer

Life is fun and full of glee
But what would life be like without TV?

Christopher Ingram (10)
St Dunstan's RC Primary School, Woking

The Snake

Slithery, slimy snake
Slowly slithers on the
Ground carefully
Trying to choose
Its prey.

Gianluca Suppa (7)
St Dunstan's RC Primary School, Woking

The Last Battle

We have no time to care for others
For visions we see that bring us but here
No time to realise what rivers we pass
We must hurry for the gobbling lord gains on us
One by one he takes us down
To see what victim he has found
Our numbers decreasing just like sound
We must go to the undying lands
And it is there that we will fight
For a glorious battle we are willing to die

The horns are blowing, the shields are up, the spears are down
Waiting for goblins to charge
Then in the south a light appeared
With the goblins marching towards us we regained hope
We ran into battle with swords high
The screaming of the goblins should soon die
With blood on my sword, I swung it right and left
Till one goblin standing, we shot him down *dead!*
We had won the battle and the goblin lord had fallen,
The free lands of men and women were once again free.

Jed Tune (10)
St Dunstan's RC Primary School, Woking

Dinner Ladies

Behind, in the kitchen, who knows what they're making,
Definitely not pudding and definitely not baking,
It could be rats
In silly hats,
Or maybe snakes
With beetle-eye cakes,
The teachers are in on it, I can tell by their faces,
Their wonky false teeth and chopped-up braces,
I hope they don't see this, I know what they'll do,
They'll make my life hell and might poison me too.

Rosanna Suppa (9)
St Dunstan's RC Primary School, Woking

What A Buffet

Food relaxed on my plate begging
to be eaten, chips sizzling, walking
out of the frying pan, jumping in
my mouth. But wait, that's not all,
we have more food to talk about
so don't stop reading.

Pizza, everybody loves pizza, it's just
gorgeous, the cheese bubbling like it's
been on the beach eating ice cream.
Pizza is delish, you can cook it and
then it will say *eat me, eat me!*
You won't believe, my pizza just jumped
off my fork and drank some of my
Coke, unbelievable.

Food is lovely, it keeps us alive,
food is what people need and it
should be treated like a king or queen
but we don't treat it like that
we scoff it in our mouth so fast
you'll be spinning.

Andrea Avellano (11)
St Dunstan's RC Primary School, Woking

The Almighty Man

There is a man who goes around and doesn't care
Slabbering and battering people he doesn't know
Scraping stitches everywhere
Injuring more and more people
Which makes his family fortune of pride glory
Bringing in arguments day by day for what he does
No one knows what his job is
But his secretive name is known as the almighty man.

Jason Trillo (10)
St Dunstan's RC Primary School, Woking

A Time Of?

Once upon a rhyme,
there was once a time.
A time of peace where no war was heard or seen.
A time where people didn't judge others by colour,
looks and appearances.
A time where everybody shared and was not left out
and when others were respected and people cared.

Nowadays we hear swearing, hate and war,
people now judge others by colour, looks and their friends.
The world has flipped over and has walked away,
now the sun does not shine anymore, it runs away
and hides beneath the clouds.
Life seems as if looks are the only thing that count.

Think for a moment,
is it nature destroying us and the world
or is it us destroying nature?

Sarah Spears (11)
St Dunstan's RC Primary School, Woking

The Looks Of The Earth

I like everything in nature
I like the way I wake up hearing the charming singing of a bird
I like the way I go outside and see a colourful butterfly
I like the way I look in the pond and find a green grass frog
I like the way I see rabbits hopping for joy

I like the hundreds of leaves on a tree
I like the red, white and yellow of flowers
I like the looks of the Earth.

Ryan Hannaford (11)
St Dunstan's RC Primary School, Woking

If An Alien Landed In My Garden

If an alien landed in my garden,
Who knows what powers we could discover then,
People would kneel down before us,
While we demolish Tony Blair.

If an alien landed in my garden,
Who knows what could happen then,
My parents could turn into zombies
And my dog would go round the bend.

If an alien walked into my garden,
Who knows what could happen then,
My teacher could do our homework
While we tip baked beans in her afternoon tea.

Charlotte Harding (10)
St Dunstan's RC Primary School, Woking

Friendship

F riends are like diamonds, they are real and rare,
R acists are like devils, they bring Hell everywhere,
I have a strong friendship with a pretty girl,
E yes like an emerald and teeth white as pearls,
N obody will break our friendship which is true,
D o you think our friendship will end, best friend is it you?
S he dances round with a spin,
H er hair blowing in the innocent wind,
I found our friendship when we met in the park,
P lease don't go, I'll be left in the dark.

Ashley Smith (10)
St Dunstan's RC Primary School, Woking

Virtual Reality

Deep in the forest,
Where creatures creep,
I stare at the trees,
There they sleep.

Then I stroll down the
Waterfall,
I peer up at the rocks,
They look so tall.

I climb up into the leafy trees,
There's where I see,
The calm,
Blue seas.

Children are walking
Back to their classes,
As I take off
My virtual reality glasses.

Rosemary Kelley (10)
St Dunstan's RC Primary School, Woking

Silence!

Everyone is awakened
By the sound of:
Buzzing bees,
Squawking birds,
Perking parrots,
Moaning canaries,
Stomping elephants

And most of all,
The king of the jungle . . .
The lion!

Michaela Moore (10)
St Dunstan's RC Primary School, Woking

Just Frisby

I'll chase my frisbee
And my ball,
Even if it goes over the garden wall.
I might not sit
When you say it,
But just me, Frisby.

I'm boisterous and bouncy,
I'm jumpy and pouncy
And after tea I'll play, you'll see,
Soon I'll get bored
And sleep in your car, Ford,
But that's just your dog, Frisby!

Jennifer Stedman (11)
St Dunstan's RC Primary School, Woking

Wind

You never ever stay away
Every day
Every day
You always come on back to me
You bring down trees
And crash the seas
You whip the people
Take a whack at steeples
Why do we like you?
We don't
You're the wind.

Mary Rogers (11)
St Dunstan's RC Primary School, Woking

Shirley The Shrimp

I live by the seaside
I moved there last week
I live at number 71
In the road called Cherry Creek

I went somewhere special yesterday
And guess where I got to be?
Right next to the seaside
Paddling in the sea

And guess who I met in the rock pool?
A tiny little shrimp
She said her name was Shirley
And the sea creatures called her a wimp

So we decided to be best friends
And I would come here every day
I'm glad I made friends with Shirley
And I hope it stays that way.

Charlotte Penn (7)
St Mary's CE Junior School, Oxted

My Dinosaur Poem

I wish I could see a real dinosaur,
I'd see a triceratops, stegosaurus,
Iguanodon and a stegoceras,
I'd see the big ones and the small ones,
The long ones and the short ones,
The fast ones and the slow ones,
The flying ones and the swimming ones,
The horned ones and the armoured ones,
The meat-eating ones and the plant-eating ones,
I'd see pentaceratops, nodosauras,
Kentrosaurus and a panoplosaurus,
I wonder which one I'd like best
If I could see a real dinosaur?

Nathan Howells (9)
St Mary's CE Junior School, Oxted

Nightmares

The flames are spitting hot,
As they overlap in fury,
They boil and bubble,
There is no way out.

The doors are sealed behind you,
The wind whirls round and round,
Bad memories return to you,
They whistle in your mind.

The dark, gloomy faces
Of ill relatives and friends
Haunt you, scare you, spook you,
You go back to tragedies.

'If you do this,' they would say,
'Your hands will stay attached!'
But if you do not . . .
You wake up in bed, sweating.

Helen Shaw (10)
St Mary's CE Junior School, Oxted

Silly Brothers And Sisters

I have a naughty sister who runs around all day making life difficult
There's nothing else to say

I also have a brother who's always that way
I wish he could be quiet for once in a day

If only they were good like me
We'd have a happy day

We'd read some books
And then we would all play.

Emma Soden (8)
St Mary's CE Junior School, Oxted

The Walk!

As we walked along the beach,
The wind blowing my hair,
He kissed me,
Oh that wonderful moment.

That moment was the best
Of its kind, my first kiss,
Oh I couldn't concentrate in school,
I received detention, my love was there!

Where will he take me
Next time we go out?
Oh my love I really can't wait,
How long will it last?

Naomi Harris (9)
St Mary's CE Junior School, Oxted

A Need For Speed

You have the need
For the speed
In a car
That will go so far!

So far away
On a very sunny day
When you have the need
For speed!

With the wind in your hair
And the purr of the car
One could travel so far
When you have the need for speed!

Jacob Willis (9)
St Mary's CE Junior School, Oxted

Mr Nobody
(Dedicated to my brother, Dan)

Who took my tooth from beneath my pillow
And left all the marks in the hall?
Who put Dad's briefcase in the crib?
Mr Nobody did it all

What's that coin shining in the baby's nappy
And why is there paint on the cat?
Who flooded the bathroom wall to wall?
Mr Nobody did it all

(I, of course, have done nothing at all!)

Tom Munns (8)
St Mary's CE Junior School, Oxted

My Rabbit

My rabbit is sweet
She loves the heat
Her name is Honey
She is such a beautiful bunny
She's a small little bun
We have so much fun
I love to sing her a song
We sit there all day long.

Natasha Phillips (9)
St Mary's CE Junior School, Oxted

A New Day

I woke to the sun rising,
The moon falling,
The birds singing,
The flowers opening,
Once again a new day,
Everything before fades away.

Portia Baker (10)
St Mary's CE Junior School, Oxted

A Peacock

A peacock has the colours of orange, blue and green
And if you look closely on the face, you might see some cream
As you know peacocks have very large tails
And if you have heard one, you know how it screeches and wails
With its proud head far from the ground
It shows us the way it is crowned
The biggest, the most beautiful bird in the world is a peacock!

Charlotte Dunn (8)
St Mary's CE Junior School, Oxted

My Cat Yoshi

I have this Burmese cat called Yoshi,
He's very cheeky and hungry like me,
Sometimes he wants to come to school,
But Mummy doesn't let him,
When he's feeling really cheeky he bites my parents' chins,
He likes to fight with Lottie
And Munchies are his favourite din-dins.

Luke Thompson (7)
St Mary's CE Junior School, Oxted

The Fairies

Fairies fly this way and that way
They fly in your bedroom and in your garden
This way and that way, every way they go
Some in the night, some in the day
They find friends to play.

Emma De Lange (7)
St Mary's CE Junior School, Oxted

The Farmyard

When I go down to the farmyard
There's so much I want to see
The bright yellow chicks that are so fluffy
And white geese that waddle about
There's a big angry bull that you mustn't let out
The speckle hens that lay lovely brown eggs
The baby white lambs with their wobbly legs
There's a friendly brown cow that gives us our milk
And tiny kittens that feel just like silk
There's a big red rooster that guards all the hens
And muddy pink pigs in their smelly old pens
There's a hardworking dog that looks after the sheep
And a friendly old donkey that I'd love to keep
The ginger farm cat that sits on my knee
Is there anything left that I've forgotten to see?

Terri Perks (9)
St Mary's CE Junior School, Oxted

My Family

The family I am in sometimes can be noisy and also very loud,
There's lots of food and drink whenever I'm allowed,
It's always warm and bright and always just right,
My mum and dad are always there making us all happy,
If only everyone had a family like mine, they would also be happy.

Sam Bowles (10)
St Mary's CE Junior School, Oxted

Norman Noodle

Norman Noodle sells nine noodles,
But nine noodles are not Norman's,
Norman can do voodoo hoodoo
And he has a puppy poodle.

Naomi Macphail (9)
St Mary's CE Junior School, Oxted

The Door
(Based on 'The Door' by Miroslav Holub)

Go on, open the door
Maybe there's a sack of gold
Maybe there's 60,000 rubies
Maybe there are three snowmen

Go on, open the door
Maybe there is some roast beef
Maybe there's a statue of a scarlet king

Go on, open the door
Maybe there's a fog
Maybe there's a magic wand with a teapot
Maybe there are five dogs

Go on, open the door
Maybe there's a TV
Maybe there's a fat cat
Open it, even if there's nothing at all!

Joshua Milne (8)
St Mary's CE Junior School, Oxted

Nocturnal Animals

Everything is quiet and the moonlight is shining on the grass,
Rustling noises are coming from the hedge,
It's a hedgehog playing with leaves!

Everything is peaceful, I can hear padding feet on the garden path,
It's a fox trying to find food!

Everything is still, I can hear digging coming from outside,
It's a badger trying to escape from his home!

Everything is silent, I look out the window,
All the animals have gone into their homes,
It's a sunny morning.

Sarah Cannon (7)
St Mary's CE Junior School, Oxted

Into The Box . . .

Into the box I will put
The slyness of a fox,
The toe of a man,
The smell of a skunk,
The wrinkles of my gran.

Into the box I will put
The nest of a magpie,
The cackle of a witch,
The cobweb of a spider,
The slime from a ditch.

Into the box I will put
The voice of a crow,
The wings of a bat,
The shadow of a ghost,
The tail from a rat.

Matthew Bristow (9)
St Mary's CE Junior School, Oxted

There's Something About The Weather . . .

I love it in May,
When it's sunny all day
And the flowers begin to open.

I hate the rain,
It's such a pain,
It gives me such a soaking.

I enjoy the snow,
I have such a glow
When I return from sledging.

Annalisa Haywood (10)
St Mary's CE Junior School, Oxted

Fairies

Fairies, fairies scuttle in the air,
Fairies, fairies everywhere,
Fairies, fairies I like them so,
Fairies, fairies so tiny, so small,
Even though I can't see them go,
I still like them so,
So next time you see one,
Let them know you like them so . . .

Kate Pugh (8)
St Mary's CE Junior School, Oxted

Apple

I eat this apple
So juicy, so sweet
'Cause I eat any apple
So round and huge
Take a big bite
Yummy and crunchy
I eat this apple
For my lunch.

Emmie Claringbull (7)
St Mary's CE Junior School, Oxted

Fly Away Butterfly

Fly away butterfly
Here comes the net
Fly away high and wide
Don't become a pet
Spirit with wings fly
High in the sky
Please don't get caught
If you do, you will die.

Alessia Tomei (9)
St Mary's CE Junior School, Oxted

Story Times

S ometimes during story times
T ony sucks his tie
O liver chews his dinosaur rubber
R obert goes cross-eyed
Y asmin eats her ponytail

T homas bites his vest
I sobel wiggles her ears round and round
M e - what do I like best?
E ating that bit of bubblegum
S omeone left under my desk.

Jordan Philip (10)
St Mary's CE Junior School, Oxted

My Dog, Toffee

My dog, Toffee
Likes to drink coffee
It's always been a mystery to me
Why she doesn't drink Coke
And she doesn't like beer
But maybe she'll like a cup of tea.

Rosie Tarrant (10)
St Mary's CE Junior School, Oxted

The Girl From France

There was a pretty girl from France,
Her brave dad had a wooden lance,
He won a huge fight,
The scared girl got a terrible fright
And then they had a lovely dance.

James Fish (9)
St Mary's CE Junior School, Oxted

Me!

I am as small as a snowman
Standing out in the cold,
As caring as a consultant
Looking after the old.

I am as blond as a beach
As the sand lies wet,
As clever as can be,
In the second maths set.

I am as sensitive as skin
When pricked with a needle,
As musical as McCartney
When he was a Beatle.

I am as helpful as a housemaid
In a Victorian house,
As quiet *in* a quarrel,
As a giant-sized mouse.

I am as busy as a bee,
Working all day,
As fast as 5G
Going out to play.

But I wish I was taller
And lived by the sea,
But other than that
I'm glad I'm *me!*

Jacob Leach (9)
St Mary's CE Junior School, Oxted

Winter - Haiku

Trickling frozen trees
Clear icicles glittering
Snowman built by child.

Anna-Leigh Casey (9)
St Mary's CE Junior School, Oxted

Dare You

Dare you to open the door
Go on! Go on!
Open the door!

Dare you,
I bet there's gold or silver
Or even leaping dolphins or
Barking whales.

Dare you,
Open it, open the door!
Go on! Go on!
Open it! Open it!
Go on!

That's it,
Lovely draught.

Matthew Williams (8)
St Mary's CE Junior School, Oxted

Pets

My pets are lovely,
They make me feel safe and sound,
Hector is a hound.

Not so long ago,
I used to have a bunny,
She was quite funny.

I don't want a cat,
They grow to be quite hairy
And a bit scary.

I'd quite like a fish,
I would put it on my plate,
Humming as I ate.

Holly Charlett (9)
St Mary's CE Junior School, Oxted

The Monster Under My Bed

That monster underneath my bed,
Has long arms and a very big head,
He wakes at night and sleeps at day,
Will he ever go away?

Don't look now, it's a scary sight,
You'll be overcome by fright!
When I go to sleep after being washed and fed,
I can hear the growling from under my bed!

Catherine Conquest (10)
St Mary's CE Junior School, Oxted

The Elephant

The elephant is a lovely bird, its fur is very soft
It doesn't fly very fast and sleeps up in the loft
It lays its eggs on the ground, when it's pouring with rain
And if they get washed away, it lays some more again
Its bark is very loud, but it does not bite
Unless you upset it then it just might
I want to get one and take it to my school
But it won't get through the door, I am a silly fool.

Molly Borer (10)
St Mary's CE Junior School, Oxted

The Hungry Dinosaur

There once was a dinosaur, Fred
Who liked nothing to eat but bread
But it had not been invented
So he grew thin and dented
And soon he was lying there dead.

Stephen Dunnell (10)
St Mary's CE Junior School, Oxted

The Beautiful Door
(Based on 'The Door' by Miroslav Holub)

Go on, open the door, it's sure to be beautiful
The door is scarlet and shimmering
Maybe inside there's a faraway tree
Which leads to a land of sweets
Like the cottage in Hansel and Gretal

Go on, open the door, maybe inside there is
A land of sport with acres of jade fields
To play golf in, with tennis courts as big as towns

Go and open the door, maybe outside there's
A land of unicorns and angels where
The angels use the clouds as trampolines
And use the stars as balls to play catch with
So whatever you do you must open the door!

Megan McGeown (8)
St Mary's CE Junior School, Oxted

The Door
(Based on 'The Door' by Miroslav Holub)

Go and open the door,
Maybe a fawn will invite you to tea,
Go on, open the door,
A sparkling city awaits,
Wind and rain last no more,
Through that pure white door,
Angels sing from the heavens above,
Beyond that snow-white door,
A land of belief and fortune, hope and faith are there to stay,
Leave the dirty world you live in,
Come and live within a new world of giving,
Through an unusual door,
If you stay, terror and death will close in,
So go and open the door,
Or the consequences lie in your path.

Faith Willsher (9)
St Mary's CE Junior School, Oxted

What's In The Jungle?

I was running through the jungle
As fast as I could go,
I heard a creepy noise
So I went on tippy-toe.

I was tippy-toeing through the jungle
As quiet as I could be,
I was looking everywhere
To see what I could see.

What can I see in the jungle,
Now what could it be?
The noise is closer now
It must be behind that tree.

The tree is in the jungle
The noise from behind that tree,
What is it? I cannot see
But can it see me?

I know what's in the jungle
I can see him and he can see me
Can you guess what's in the jungle?
My imagination silly, *it's only me!*

Danielle Herpe (10)
St Mary's CE Junior School, Oxted

The Jungle

The creeping weeds,
The marvellous trees,
This is what the jungle heeds.

The most beautiful birds
Can clearly be heard
From miles away on the leaves.

The wonderful sights,
The dizzying heights,
The insects will give you nasty *bites!*

David Swift (10)
St Mary's CE Junior School, Oxted

Winter

When the days get colder,
What do we do?
We wrap up in hats and scarves.
In the winter
It may snow,
You never, never know,
That may be you out in that snow!
Building snowmen,
Throwing snowballs,
Ice skating too.
Believe in your dreams,
Then they will come true!

Genevieve Cox (7)
St Mary's CE Junior School, Oxted

Digging

Digging at the beach,
Searching for buried treasure,
Thinking what you'll find.

Digging in the caves,
Looking for ancient fossils,
Thinking what you'll find.

Digging in a field,
Searching for rare stones,
Thinking what you'll find.

But who knows what I might find,
Just digging in my garden.

William Houghton (9)
St Mary's CE Junior School, Oxted

The Ice Cream Door
(Based on 'The Door' by Miroslav Holub)

Go on, open the sapphire door
Maybe there will be
An ice cream seller
And the ice cream is
Free and every flavour

Go on, open the sapphire door
Maybe there will be a mound
Of chocolate ice cream with
Sprinkles and the sun in the sky

Go on, open the emerald door
Maybe there will be a huge
Bowl of toffee ice cream
And chocolate sauce and
The reflection of the sun

Go on, open the golden door
Maybe there will be a massive
Ice cream cone with hundreds
And thousands piled on top

Open the door if I were you.

George Jensen (9)
St Mary's CE Junior School, Oxted

Open The Door
(Based on 'The Door' by Miroslav Holub)

Go on, open the door
Maybe there's a garden with pretty
Flowers or a jungle

Go on, open the door
Maybe there's a pony or a dog
Go on, open the door
Maybe there's plants growing up fences
And up the greenhouse.

Alice Brock (8)
St Mary's CE Junior School, Oxted

Lunch

My lunch is too big
My lunch is too small
My dad never gets it right
But he always gets it wrong

Yuck grapes!
Yuck cucumber!
Mmm KitKat
Mmm sausage sandwiches
Mmm ham and pickle
Mmm cheese and pickle
Mum put it in

Sausage sandwich
Salt 'n' vinegar crisps and a KitKat
It is a shame Mum does not do it every day.

William Greenland (9)
St Mary's CE Junior School, Oxted

The Cool Door

Go and open the door
I bet you, it's copper or gold
It might have violet marigolds
So go and open the door
It's filled with sweets and money
And all you could wish for
Or a magic world with a man
A man that is charming

So go on
So go on
So go on.

Laura Dennison (8)
St Mary's CE Junior School, Oxted

The Door
(Based on 'The Door' by Miroslav Holub)

Go on, open the door
Maybe there's angels
Open the door
Maybe there's a rainbow

Go on, open the door
Maybe there's gold sand
Open the door
Maybe there's a castle

Go on, open the door
Maybe there's trees and hills
Open the door
Maybe there's a stream

Go on, open the door
Maybe there's an apple tree
Open the door
Maybe there's God's kingdom

Go on, open the door
Just open the ruby-red door.

Thomas Saunders (9)
St Mary's CE Junior School, Oxted

The Lime-Green Door
(Based on 'The Door' by Miroslav Holub)

Open the lime-green door
There might be a big bowl of cherries
There might be the biggest box of toffees in the world
Open the lime-green door
There might be an elephant playing the drums
There might be a magic mountain
Open the lime-green door
There might be a kingdom made of marshmallows
There might be 100,000,000 rubies
Open the door, it's lovely.

Jack Poole (8)
St Mary's CE Junior School, Oxted

Open The Door
(Based on 'The Door' by Miroslav Holub)

Go on, open the emerald and ruby door,
Go on, open it, there could be a chocolate factory,
There could be a candy mountain
Or a liquorice rainbow,
You never know, so open it.

Open the door,
It could have hills of green,
Or there could be a beautiful sand island,
You could find angels with harps,
You never know, so open it.

Go on, open the door,
There could be a palace,
Or a magic wand,
It could be a dream come true,
Go on, open it, it's your only chance,
Open it, now or never.

Meghan Sharp (9)
St Mary's CE Junior School, Oxted

The Door
(Based on 'The Door' by Miroslav Holub)

Go on, open the door, maybe there's a fluffy bunny,
Maybe a field of roses,
Go and open the door, maybe there's a garden of opera,
Maybe a disco,
Go and open the door, maybe there's a jar of liquorice,
Maybe a generous old lady,
Go and open the door, maybe there's a cup of tea,
Maybe an apple tree,
Go and open the door, maybe there's a rainbow,
Maybe a pot of gold.

Please open the door!

Georgina Bashford (9)
St Mary's CE Junior School, Oxted

The Door
(Based on 'The Door' by Miroslav Holub)

Go on, open the buttercup door
Maybe there's a free ice cream shop
Or an opera free ticket

Go on, open the door
Maybe there's a mulberry dragon
Or even a peach lizard

Go on, open the chestnut-stripped door
Maybe there's a honey-coloured teddy bear
Or even a sapphire land

Go on, open the door
Maybe there's a lime land
Or even a jade city

Go on, open the door
Maybe there's a ruby helmet
Or a smoky, staley, huge dock

Go now and open the door.

Alice Dickerson (9)
St Mary's CE Junior School, Oxted

The Door
(Inspired by 'The Door' by Miroslav Holub)

Get in the door,
Maybe there's some bats squealing in your ears
Or a goblin waiting for its food, dribbling saliva down its thrusty throat,
Or even a psycho policeman with guns

I said get in there
Maybe there's a grave with a pale spiky hand sticking out
Or some vampires with pointy vicious fangs feeding
                                                 on people's brains!

Get in there!

Dominic Nolan (9)
St Mary's CE Junior School, Oxted

The Door
(Based on 'The Door' by Miroslav Holub)

Go on, open the door,
Maybe the door is in a magic wood,
Maybe the door is scarlet-red with flowers around it.

Go on, open the door,
Maybe there is a sapphire-blue sky with a bright sun,
Maybe there's a mountain of scrumptious sweets.

Go on, open the door,
Maybe there's an empty beach with golden sand,
Maybe there's a beautiful rainbow with fluttering fairies.

Go on, open the door,
Maybe there's a lovely garden with so many flowers,
Maybe there's a dark sky with a bright moonlight.

Emily Murphy (9)
St Mary's CE Junior School, Oxted

The Dark Door
(Inspired by 'The Door' by Miroslav Holub)

Dare you to open the door
You never know what's behind the door
Maybe chocolate land
Maybe a passage to a two-dimensional world
But whatever you do, you must open the door,

Dare you to open the door
Maybe a bloodsucking vampire bat
Maybe a door to another door
But whatever you do you must open the door.

Simon Barker (9)
St Mary's CE Junior School, Oxted

I Can't Swim

I can't swim and I can't dive,
But this time . . . I tried.
I climbed up the diving board
The highest one it was
I took the plunge straight away
I was in a cloud of fog

I hit the floor in five seconds or more
I think I did a rollover
All I need now is a lucky four-leafed clover!
I swam up and gasped for breath
Mum picked me up and said I needed a rest
But I was excited
I swam!

Lauren Franklin (8)
St Mary's CE Junior School, Oxted

Wish, Wish, Wish

I wish that I had long hair,
I wish I had a cuddly bear,
I wish I had straight teeth,
I wish that I had a wreath.

I wish my hair was curly,
I wish I had a Curly Wurly
I wish I had high heels
I wish I had a cart with wheels

I wish I could stay up late
I wish I had choc on my plate
I wish I had a car
I wish I had a bar
I wish I had a phone.

Kenna Courtman (8)
St Mary's CE Junior School, Oxted

Zoo

Tigers prowling,
    Warthogs scowling,
        Dolphins flipping,
            Kangaroos kicking.

Penguins waddling,
    Macaws squabbling,
        Lions roaring,
            Vultures soaring.

Cheetahs racing,
    Feet pacing,
        Monkeys swinging,
            Ears ringing.

With the sound of the
Zoo!

Eleanor Fox (8)
St Mary's CE Junior School, Oxted

I Wish

I wish I had my ears pierced,
I wish I had a phone,
I wish I had a bigger room,
Not much I want, I know.

I wish I had a kitten,
I wish I had a horse,
I wish I had a puppy,
How many?
Four of course.

Sarah Barratt (9)
St Mary's CE Junior School, Oxted

Football

I wish I had Zidane's skill
I wish I could swing in crosses like David Beckham
I wish I had speed of Henry
I wish I had the saves of Nigel Martyn
I wish I had the shot of Michael Owen
I wish I had the tackling skills of Sol Campbell
I wish I had the left foot of Roberto Carlos
And then you would have the ultimate footballer.

Nicholas Burns (9)
St Mary's CE Junior School, Oxted

I Wish

I wish my brother was kind,
I wish I could see in my mind.
I wish the water was clear,
I wish I could fix my broken ear.

I wish my friends were always nice,
I wish I was a pop spice.
I wish I didn't have to tidy my room,
I wish, I wish, I wish!

Bronwen Craft (8)
St Mary's CE Junior School, Oxted

I Wish

I wish I had a pet,
A bunny or a dog,
But what I really want to get
Is a kitten called Mog.

I'll act just like their mummy,
I'll be really good,
I would feed his hungry tummy,
As good friends should.

Emma Moss (8)
St Mary's CE Junior School, Oxted

The Rosy Red Door
(Based on 'The Door' by Miroslav Holub)

Go on, open the rosy red door,
Perhaps there's a tree or more,
Perhaps there's a unicorn sliding down a rainbow,
As far ahead as you can go,
Perhaps there's swaying grass
And a band of musical brass.

Go on, open the door.
Maybe there's a snake in the grass,
Or a lizard sunning itself on the path,
Maybe there's a warm breeze,
From your head to your knees.

Hannah Turner (8)
St Mary's CE Junior School, Oxted

I Am A Friend To Others

I am a friend to others
I wonder what it is like in Heaven
I hear birds chirping
I see leaves falling to the ground
I want the world to be friendly
I am a friend to others

I pretend to float
I feel the leaves slipping through my palms
I worry I will be poked by a twig
I cry when I am injured
I am a friend to others

I understand nobody is perfect
I say I love art
I dream most things can happen if you make them
I hope
I am.

Nicole Norman (10)
TASIS - The American School In England, Thorpe

A Problem

I have a great big problem
and it's growing every day.
I want to pull my hair out,
but my problem's here to stay.

It came to me at Christmas,
when Santa came around.
This problem sat beneath the tree,
while Santa crept around.

Christmas morning I was counting gifts,
but only *one* displayed my name.
The biggest box beneath the tree,
was *mine,* I felt like fame!

I opened up my present
and laid bare upon my knees,
the biggest pile you've ever seen
of videos and DVDs.

I got all the latest titles,
most were not in theatres yet.
I could hardly wait to show my friends,
they'd be jealous you could bet!

Then my mum looked at my bounty
and my problem came to light.
She sighed her great big 'mother sigh'
and crossed her arms real tight.

'Let me remind you of our TV rule,'
Mum said while standing tall.
'Since your grades are low and lacking,
you've not got TV allowed at all.'

My chin began to quiver
and my eyes began to cry.
'Oh Mum, you can't be serious?
No TV *now* and I shall die!'

But Mum stood firm and wouldn't bend,
she wouldn't change her tune.
She said, 'Just put those in your room,
you know school is out in June!'

So here I sit with my problem,
of videos and DVDs.
There's not a lot of use for them,
if you aren't allowed TV.

Olivia Krutz (11)
TASIS - The American School In England, Thorpe

I Am A Cool Person

I wonder about other parts of the world
I hear my friends chatting
I see my TV
I want a puppy
I am a cool person

I pretend that I am the queen of the world
I feel happy when I am with my friends
I touch my hair to make it perfect
I worry about having a maths test
I cry when I hurt myself badly
I am a cool person

I understand I have to clean my bedroom
I say nice things to my friends
I dream that I am queen of the world
I try to be queen of the world
I hope to be queen of the world
I am a cool person.

Jaimee Gundry (9)
TASIS - The American School In England, Thorpe

I Am Happy

I am happy
I wonder about my grades
I hear my mum
I see my TV
I want a dog
I am happy

I pretend to be a sparkly devil
I feel my hair
I touch a pencil
I worry about pollution
I cry when I get hurt
I am happy

I understand about brothers
I say hello
I dream about my life
I try to be good at maths
I hope to make friends
I am happy.

Megan Yeigh (9)
TASIS - The American School In England, Thorpe

I Am Nine Years Old

I am nine years old
I wonder how many people live on Earth
I hear birds every morning
I see deer every morning
I want a snowy Christmas
I am nine years old

I pretend to be a soldier
I feel very happy
I touch the pencil to the paper
I worry about maths tests
I cry when I get mad
I am nine years old

I understand all kinds of sports
I say the right answer
I dream about different worlds
I try to be nice to my sister
I hope to play sports when I get older
I am nine years old.

Dylan Bole (10)
TASIS - The American School In England, Thorpe

I Am A Curious Girl

I am a curious girl
I wonder about the world around me
I hear the people around me
I see the computer in front of me
I want to travel the world
I am a curious girl

I pretend that I can fly
I feel my books
I touch my life as it expands
I worry about when my grandfather will die
I cry when I am badly hurt
I am a curious girl

I understand complicated things
I say I love my cat
I dream of a faraway place
I try to do my best in school
I hope I live a long, great life
I am a curious girl.

Anneliese Rinaldi (9)
TASIS - The American School In England, Thorpe

I Am An Exciting Boy

I am an exciting boy
I wonder what it will be like when I grow up
I hear my dogs barking
I see a football in the air
I want a happy, healthy long life
I am an exciting boy

I pretend to be a football player
I feel strong
I touch a football
I worry about my spelling test
I cry when I get hurt badly
I am an exciting boy

I understand maths
I say I'm happy
I dream I'm a professional football player
I try to have fun
I hope I will live long
I am an exciting boy.

Kyle Andersen (9)
TASIS - The American School In England, Thorpe

I Am A Girl

I am a girl
I wonder if I will ever get a dog
I hear birds
I see trees
I want a dog
I am a girl

I pretend to sleep
I feel my books
I touch my bed
I cry when I get hurt
I am a girl

I understand books
I say I want a dog
I dream that I have a dog
I try to read The Hobbit
I hope I will get a dog
I am a girl.

Maggie Seymour (10)
TASIS - The American School In England, Thorpe

Erosion

Wearing away swiftly, silently too,
Opening up rock, to us anew,
The world is always changing, right underneath our feet,
But only for some things we can make ends meet,
Here at school friends come and go,
This I know is so,
Erosion is wearing the rock away,
Be careful, it might be us someday.

Kathryn Meyer (11)
TASIS - The American School In England, Thorpe

I Am A Baseball Player

I am a baseball player
I wonder how my body works
I hear my dog barking
I see Andy mowing the soccer field
I want another dog
I am a baseball player

I pretend to be a baseball player
I feel like reading
I touch my homework
I worry that there will be a war
I cry when I get badly hurt
I am a baseball player

I understand that you learn from your mistakes
I say hello to people
I dream of being a baseball player
I try to do my best
I hope that I will be a major league baseball player.

Timmy Davison (9)
TASIS - The American School In England, Thorpe

The Aliens

Mummy, today I went to the Planet Zorg where I saw some
aliens speaking Zog. They blurted and blahhed until I was bored
and ran over to see a Zag match. Suddenly some Zuxs with
laser guns came up to tell me they wanted my guts!
I went to their leader who was a terrible sight
and was very keen on being mean to earthlings at Zorg.
So Mummy, that's why I left school early
can you never send me back because they'll know it's me
and make me flee and never come back!

Martin Sartorius (11)
TASIS - The American School In England, Thorpe

Wanted

Old and grumpy witches
Old and grumpy witches are:
Weird, mean, ugly and fat.
They have:
Big noses, tangled hair, long fingernails and bloodshot eyes,
Lizard-like tongues, big fat cheeks as round as baseballs,
Long pointy toes and pimples and warts all over their faces.
They own:
Black cats, pointy hats and shoes, a broomstick, a cauldron
And of course a wand, but never forget that they eat little children
Small and big, that they feed them frogs and mites
And everything bad, but never ever, ever forget that they live in
A crooked house that has dark clouds above it that rain non-stop
But remember that they live on top of a dark, dark hill
In a dark, dark country.

So if you see one, please report it!

£100 dead, £1,000 alive with black cat.

Dominique Saayman (10)
TASIS - The American School In England, Thorpe

The Perfect Place

I look up at the sky on a cold winter's night,
All the stars are shining bright,
I see my breath in front of my face,
And wonder if there could be a more beautiful place.
I feel like I'm in a dream,
It's so quiet I can't even scream,
I look at the facts,
I'm stuck in my tracks,
It's hard to go,
So I go so slow.

Lauryn Dichting (10)
TASIS - The American School In England, Thorpe

Bubblegum

Bubblegum - smugglegum - lugglegum
The best flavours in the world
It's the chewiest, gooiest gum
It comes in every colour of the world
Bubblegum - smugglegum - lugglegum

Bubblegum - smugglegum - lugglegum
I went and bought me some
It was good, yum, yum, yum
I kept it in my mouth all night
So I could taste it in my sleep
Bubblegum - smugglegum - lugglegum

Bubblegum - smugglegum - lugglegum
I woke up in the morning
And my mouth was glued shut
I tried many things to get it off
I tried to dissolve it with water
I tried to set it on fire
So I could burn it off
I went to the dentist
But they couldn't get it off
So I am stuck here
With my mouth glued tight
For the rest of me life all because of
Bubblegum - smugglegum - lugglegum.

Sarah Lawhon (10)
TASIS - The American School In England, Thorpe

A Friendly Letter

Dear Mr Whatsyourname,
A better name for you:
Lame brain, same game,
Maybe even Goo.
Dear Mr Whatsyourname,
Thank you for your letter
And thank you for your phone number,
This is getting even better.
I will call you soon,
Any day now,
So be ready for the phone to ring.
Dear Mr Whatsyourname,
Have you heard the news?
I'm your next-door neighbour,
So be sure to watch out,
I'll have you when you least expect me,
You'll see!
PS You'd better not own any garlic!

Thurston Smalley (11)
TASIS - The American School In England, Thorpe

Pineapples

So sweet
It's just a little treat
How beautiful it is
Prickling, tickling
As you try to have it as a treat
So goodbye my sweet for I will not have you as my treat
For you are the best and there is no other fruit as good as you
I guess you want to know what it is
Well, check out the headline
For you might just find out.

Alexander Larsson (10)
TASIS - The American School In England, Thorpe

Rain, Rain

Rain, rain you think it's a pain,
But from the water cycle
Rain's not all you gain.

Rain is a form of precipitation,
That forms from condensation,
That you receive from rivers, lakes, seas,
Oceans and bays.

From these water sources,
The water evaporates of courses,
Making clouds - cumulus or stratus,
White clouds or grey.

Rain, rain you think it's a pain,
But next time it rains
Think what it gives to us.

Griffin Leeds (11)
TASIS - The American School In England, Thorpe

Teddy Bear

Teddy bear, oh teddy bear
Sitting on the rocking chair,
Your ear is ripped, you have a tear
And stains from when you ate a pear.

When I got you nice and new,
You were fuzzy and stuffed, all the way through,
But when we were painting, your paw turned blue
And how it happened, we never knew.

Your eye fell out in the doctor game,
Out of your leg, some stuffing came,
So now your left leg is lame,
But I love you just the same!

Mary Buswell (11)
TASIS - The American School In England, Thorpe

I Am A Smart Girl

I am a smart girl
I wonder if I'm going to pass the grade
I hear birds singing
I see trees
I want to be good at math
I am a smart girl.

I pretend I'm a pirate
I feel happy
I touch my desk
I worry if I am going to get an A+ in my math test
I cry when I'm hurt
I am a smart girl.

I understand friendship
I say I like to read
I dream I will be famous
I try to be good at math
I hope I am a scientist
I am a smart girl.

Sofia Leiva (10)
TASIS - The American School In England, Thorpe

My Shot

I'm sitting in the waiting room with kids before the yelp
I'm here to get a booster shot, oh please Lord give me help
It's going to be terrible
It will be the death of me
I'm crying to my mum saying, 'Please don't let them kill me'
Now it is my turn, I think I'm going to faint
Now, I'm in the office room with walls of blood-red paint
The nurse comes in and holds me
Now I'm turning pale
Across my face I wear a frown
But at least I'm here to tell the tale.

Emily Goode (11)
TASIS - The American School In England, Thorpe

Sprouts

Monsters are scary,
But none are as scary as the one that guards dessert.
It's green and fearsome,
It makes me tearsome,
To watch it patrol the plate,
For it was created by a mum,
A mad scientist.

It's not very nice,
Unlike my mice,
For I'd rather kill a dragon,
Or be attacked by lice,
I'm armed with a fork and a knife,
For I must slay it,
To save my chocolate ice.

Charge!
It's the attack of the Brussels sprout,
It must go in your mouth
And not come out,
For I must slay a Brussels sprout.

Victory!
The sprout is dead,
I get dessert,
Yes, yes, yes,
Yes, yes,
Burp!

Matthew Buswell (9)
TASIS - The American School In England, Thorpe

I Am Alex

I am Alex
I wonder about aeroplanes
I hear the supersonic Concorde
I see planes everywhere
I want a big black grand piano
I am Alex

I pretend to be a pilot
I feel happy to play my piano
I touch the ground
I worry about nightmares
I cry when my brothers tell tales
I am Alex

I understand that you can't fly a plane into space
I say I want to go play with my friends
I dream about flying Concorde
I try not to do naughty things
I hope I make more friends in the future
I am Alex.

Alex Valvano (10)
TASIS - The American School In England, Thorpe

I Am A Hockey Player

I am a hockey player
I wonder if I will ever see a tiger
I hear my mum yelling
I see a computer
I want a little brother
I am a hockey player

I pretend to be a hockey player
I feel a mouse on a computer
I touch a pencil
I worry if I will die
I cry when I think about dying
I am a hockey player

I understand my dad
I say 'Hi'
I dream about people
I try to read I hope to pass the grade
I am a hockey player.

Matthew Bayern (9)
TASIS - The American School In England, Thorpe

The Big War

Romans are coming on turquoise seas
Waves like leaping dolphins
Romans came in 80 dazzling ships

Suddenly stopping! On they stepped
Atop sandy dunes
Stared at the Celts
Blue markings on bare chests.

Olivia Kenning (8)
Whyteleafe Primary School, Whyteleafe

The Dancing Snowflake

The sky turned grey,
I knew that was it.
The air turned to frost,
My journey had begun.
Wind whistled and blew about,
A biting chill hung in the air, ready to attack the first soul
To step into the empty streets,
My time had come,
I tiptoed softly over the edge of my cloud,
I started to fall slowly,
Down, down, down,
Below lay a white sheet of snow,
Awaiting my arrival,
As I pirouetted towards my friends,
I heard the creak of a door
And footsteps crunching on the glistening blanket of snow
Beneath my feet,
My pirouettes turned into an arabesque,
My feet were barely touching the ground.

As I lay on my back I saw my family
Rushing down to meet me,
However much I loved it there
I knew it was not for long,
Soon the sun would come out,
We would fade,
Sinking into the ground,
Until we were nothing more,
Than a memory.

Jessica Day (10)
Whyteleafe Primary School, Whyteleafe

My Death (Snowman)

I was born on Tuesday,
By Thursday I couldn't get to sleep,
The cold breeze gave me a slap in the face,
The snow was snoozing, lucky him.

My thin arms were weak,
They were drooping, they were upset.

My hat was cold,
My ribbon had started to become ice,
The top of my hat was falling in,
It was full of snow.

My head slipped,
It tumbled down,
Finally crashing to the ground.

Then my scarf,
It dropped to the ground swiftly.

My tummy was brittle,
I hoped and prayed it would stay,
I knew the end was soon,
My tummy toppled down.

That was the end of me,
Maybe I'll be back,
Who knows?

Sarah Hugill (10)
Whyteleafe Primary School, Whyteleafe

Beautiful Mistake

You're a beautiful mistake
I was never meant to make
Made my heart die
Left me to cry
Rain splashes down my face
Love is just a wicked race
For life

I'm now alone
Wishing
Wishing I was somewhere else
Not here
You used and abandoned me
The gloomy face of mine rains
As your bright happy face shines

There
There you are.

Tabby Campbell (10)
Whyteleafe Primary School, Whyteleafe

The Snow Dancer

I was awake all night,
Looking down from the skies above,
Peering through the swirling grey mist,
The air turned frosty,
My journey was about to begin.

My journey had begun,
I started pirouetting down slowly,
Swiftly onto the soft, white, glistening bed of pearls,
The dusk began to break.

My journey had ended,
The dawn began to break,
I gradually melted at a snail's pace.

Georgia Harbour (10)
Whyteleafe Primary School, Whyteleafe

Glimmering Like Ice

I am cold as snow
My eyes are as shiny as diamonds
I like to tease children
So they fall into my ice-cold water

The devastation I cause is bad
Normally I am snow-white
But sometimes I disguise myself
Black as can be
That's when they fear me most

It is no fun though
I have skid marks all over my face
Stinging from hot tyres
And very often I meet death
That's the bad part of being ice

As the sun rises
I hear myself cracking and creaking
The cruel sun brings the rage of Icarus
And then I'm gone.

Declan Bellingham (9)
Whyteleafe Primary School, Whyteleafe

The Invaders Are Coming

Rotten Romans are coming
What are we going to do?
Rotten Romans are coming
We are going to war

They're on the shore
What are we going to do?
Here they come
Red and gold shields
Javelins, spear-like
Arrowing upwards
What are we going to do?

Spencer Hall (8)
Whyteleafe Primary School, Whyteleafe

Death Of A Snowman

I was awake all night
The wind lashing across my face
The snow was falling as gently as a fluttering baby bird
Snowflakes falling through the winter's air

Then my bones started to turn to jelly
And I shed a tear or two
My nose started to drip
I started to grow old and hunch over

People started to forget about me
I was slowly collapsing onto the ground
There was no funeral or gravestone for me
All that was left to mark the place where I stood was my hat and scarf.

David Hopkins (9)
Whyteleafe Primary School, Whyteleafe

The Winter Ghost

A winter chill has struck the village,
Windows frozen up,
Roofs of houses coated white,
Children all wrapped up,
Mothers lighting fires bright,
Mugs of cocoa steaming hot,
Stand waiting on the table.

Snowmen standing, staring strangely,
Whilst the winter ghost sends shivers down my back,
Icicles hanging down like daggers pointing,
The winter breeze is blowing
And still the snow keeps falling,
Like a curse upon the world.

Amy Pocock (9)
Whyteleafe Primary School, Whyteleafe

Summer, Please Come Back Soon!

I've been waiting, waiting all year for this and it has arrived.
Let's have a warm welcome for the one and only *summer!*

The time when children play merrily in the empty streets
And when the fat old grannies relax in their tight red polka dot bikinis.
The unbearable heat beaming down on us,
Melting our cola ice lollies (delicious).
Young couples making love in their air-conditioned BMWs,
Dogs playing a lively game of chase.
Children of the age of 5, learning to ride their miniscule bikes
And of course family, the people who saw you take your first steps
All around you, never leaving your side.
But soon summer gets booted out and winter takes over,
Its cold hands lay a soft white sheet over the landscape.
It dribbles onto the evergreen trees so they're no longer green.
The old grannies shiver, obviously still freezing,
Even though they're wearing about one million layers.
The dogs lie still, not even moving at the sight of food.
Birds starving and snuggling together to keep warm.
Hot chocolate and soup is the only remaining heat around.
Then there's family, having to go to work
And having to drive in the terrible weather conditions,
But what gets me down in winter is *school!*
I'd much rather be at home having a tea party with
Jim-Jam my toy giraffe.
Summer, please come back soon!

Sophie Brown (10)
Whyteleafe Primary School, Whyteleafe

Snow And Rain

The wind whispers softly
while the ground lies waiting.
As the first flake lands with a soft thud
the rest come running down.
The light brings bags of joy to all
everyone comes out to play.
Darkness beckons trouble
to hide from the joyful day.
The day's end comes near,
snow turns to rain.
The children go inside
and wait for it to snow again.

The icy blanket lays soft as a pillow
on the dusty ground.
The silence falls with a graceful swoop
the carol singers go round in a group.
The moon gently breathes its beam of light
over the blanket of snow.
All the children close their eyes and wait,
for Santa to come and go.

The new day comes around the bend,
the sun comes out.
The snow turns to water,
the birds start to sing.
The children still come out to play
because it has turned to spring.

Tom Simpson (10)
Whyteleafe Primary School, Whyteleafe

Lord Of The Rings Middle-Earth

No one knows what lies ahead
When sun has faded, moon is dead
And all the Orcs on the battle plains have fled

Thread by thread they're on their way
At the Prancing Pony you have to pay
Whether you visit or stay

Galadriel gave the Lorithen light
And on their way Orcs they will have to fight

The dead fight for the living
That means we're certain to win this battle

Frodo and Sam move closer to Mount Doom
While the catapults of the Orcs break the walls
Of Minas Tirith with a boom

We have drawn his army to the black gate
Which our friendship will be at bate
And we know we'll have to use it
And fight side by side like a mate

Finally our quest is complete
And we return to our homes
Where our worrying brides moan

Now Frodo and Bilbo travel to the grey havens for everlasting life
But Bilbo worries about his slit of a knife.

Adam Foster (10)
Whyteleafe Primary School, Whyteleafe

Lord Of The Rings

The war has begun now,
It will not stop,
All our hope lies with the unlikely,
But if he fails, all hope is lost.

Yet the shire folk are unwise,
Of the trouble that lies,
But for four Hobbits their mission has begun,
They will travel through wind, rain and sun.

They seek shelter in the Prancing Pony,
Yet they have trouble with Black Riders,
The ring, they seek,
They have no hope or soul.

Aragorn will be their guide,
He wants them to hide,
The black riders sought and found,
They lay their blow on Frodo.

At Rivendell Frodo found
He was safe and sound,
His wound would never heal,
But that was nothing for what they will have to deal,
A fellowship was born.

Moria was a deadly path,
Where Durin's Bane lay with wrath,
Gandalf the Grey lay here,
Who the fellowship held dear.

The creature Gollum took Frodo along a path,
Where light was dead,
Yet Sam came in his stead,
The spider Shelob lay her wrath on Sam,
But his victory was in the can.

Matthew Urquhart (10)
Whyteleafe Primary School, Whyteleafe

The Journey

They do not know what lies ahead
They may travel through the paths of dead

They travel to find a ray of hope or light
But on their way they must fight

Even though they are brave
They don't know their danger is grave

On the boat the muscular men swish oars
Do they know they will fight many wars?

Then you see the flying dove
Going over the dead which many love

All this happening in one sad land
Can't the leaders be friends and just shake hands?

As they travel over the giant hill
Many they do have to kill

And as the families cry at their sad woe
Soldiers fight their fearsome foe.

Jacob Boitel-Gill (10)
Whyteleafe Primary School, Whyteleafe

Rotten Romans

80 sails are coming towards us,
Daggers and javelins soaring through space,
Caterpillars crawling over great big waves,
Coming to battle and seize our land.

Swords soaring, shields protecting,
Great storm cats crying,
Romans' terrifying shouts,
Time goes by.

They're attacking us bare,
With frightening armour,
Killing to win,
They won't give up.

Sophie Read (8)
Whyteleafe Primary School, Whyteleafe

The Night Alone

The hall lights suddenly became nothing,
Just a maniac house in the middle of the night.
I stroked my cat,
As I sat
Up in bed
And said,
'It's dark,
A mark,
That shows the path to noises.'

The owls
With howls,
As strong as the wind,
The foxes in the bin,
Savaging for just one tin

And the tree
Haunted me,
As the teenagers chattered,
They thought that's all that mattered.
All I know is that the night wasn't alone.

Georgina Barnard (11)
Whyteleafe Primary School, Whyteleafe

The Fierce, Ferocious Romans

Romans are ready, coming to battle
We can't stop them, they want our land
They're coming on seas, with white horse waves
Triangle sails, swiftly moving in the distance

Swords swording, shields shielding
Romans being a nuisance
Shouting and screaming, fighting and seizing
Fighting with bare chests, swords, armour and all
Silver hats and crimson hair.

Victoria Bradford (9)
Whyteleafe Primary School, Whyteleafe

Snowflake

For I am the snowflake
Drifting, drifting
No one noticed when I gave a sharp cold shriek

The white grass whistled
And the cold tree shook its branches

But now morning came and the sun is waking up
The hot sun scorched my snowy skin

I drifted to the ground
Melting, melting

Now I was small and I was
Dying, dying

I lay there as I joined the heavens of Earth
For I am the snowflake
Drifting, drifting.

Rebecca Burr (10)
Whyteleafe Primary School, Whyteleafe

Snow

In dark, lonely winter, the white wizard comes
Spreading the obedient snow everywhere
It floats down elegantly
Onto the waiting rooftops of the nearby town
Delicate, sparkling icicles hanging from the windowpanes
Snowmen made by the happy children with ruby-red cheeks
Snow, snow, snow

Still lakes and quiet ponds frozen over
Thin ice, thick ice, any will do
The piercing, icy winds bring a colour to your face
The biting snow lies on the dead, silent trees
Treating them like hard beaten slaves
Snow, oh! so deadly, snow.

Amy Knott (9)
Whyteleafe Primary School, Whyteleafe

Snow

Snow on the fields, the trees, the houses,
White on the mountains and the hills,
I wake and peep out the frosty window,
Wow!
Snow!
Rush, rush, change, run downstairs,
Scoff my toast, spill my tea,
I'm out in the snow.
Snow on the fields, the trees, the houses,
White on the mountains and the hills,
Shall I have a snowball fight
Or make a snowman?
Sledging?
Call my friends, go skating on the icy pond?
Stop.
Snow on the fields, the trees, the houses,
White on the mountains and the hills,
Look at the scenery,
Snow-coated trees like a blanket of chill,
Sparkling,
Powdery, frosty, glistening leaves on the ground.
Snow on the fields, the trees, the houses,
White on the mountains and the hills,
Icicles hanging from rooftops,
Smokey clouds, puffing from the chimneys,
Snowmen standing lonely, sad,
Soon melting in the glowing sun, say goodbye.
Snow on the fields, the trees, the houses,
White on the mountains and the hills,
Yawn,
Open the curtains,
It's gone!
Puddles everywhere!
Dripping, grey slush!
No snow on the fields, the trees, the houses,
Grass on the mountains and the hills.

Amber Cunningham (9)
Whyteleafe Primary School, Whyteleafe

A Tale Of A Survivor

I looked up at the clouds one day,
Enjoying the magnificent view.
Suddenly, they fell in chunks,
I felt deathly cold.

My mum came out and saw me,
Gazing at the sky.
She put her arms round me and said,
'It's snowing, son!'

'Snow, snow!' I said.
I held my hands out,
For the floating flakes to rest on,
For the white friends to build up on.

I ran in circles,
Making footprints,
Then the enemy of the snow appeared -
The sun . . .

My kingdom of snow was melting,
My throne was growing small.
As for my buddies,
Where were they?

I saved one though,
I named him: Survivor.
He lives in the freezer,
Nice and cold.
Maybe next winter,
I can reunite him,
With snow.

Peter Bowdery (9)
Whyteleafe Primary School, Whyteleafe

The Night White Bear

Night fell, I proudly crept out of the dark sky cave,
I stretched out my fur to make a soft fluffy pile.
I called it snow,
Children played all over me,
Ripping fur off me
And throwing it around.
What is the meaning of this?
So I fluffed up my fur
And wrapped it around me,
I was about to leap at them,
When the sun came out,
Stop!
Fragile, I ran to my cave foot by foot,
Hand by hand.
Gone!

Sophie Knox (9)
Whyteleafe Primary School, Whyteleafe

Romans Are Coming

Romans sailing on 80 dazzling ships
Romans ready for war
Celts know nothing about a Roman invasion
Spears glinting in the sun

Romans in Britannia
Celts wear blue paint
Romans as fierce as this
Celts see silver glinting armour

Celts are not scared of Romans
Romans see blue paint on Celts' bodies
Swords and shields heading straight
Boudicca is leader.

Joanna Slevin (8)
Whyteleafe Primary School, Whyteleafe

Snowman

I fall onto the garden chair,
Twinkling, shining in the air.

The children come out and play
And build me on one snowy day.

In the night I shiver and freeze,
Trees are swaying in the cool breeze.

Next day when the children come
And I am taller than everyone.

Once again the night comes round,
I slowly fall onto the ground.

Next morning the children see me lying there,
Soon I will go and disappear.

When the sun comes around
I slowly fall onto the ground.

Katie Sheldon (10)
Whyteleafe Primary School, Whyteleafe

Sudden Death

The Roman Empire
Julius Caesar strikes again
Destroying Celtic life
Killing Queen Boudicca
Never to be seen
Caesar strikes again!
Romans are here
With swords and shields
Hundreds of warriors
Fighting for a country
Risking their precious lives
Romans are here!

Jasmine C Butler (9)
Whyteleafe Primary School, Whyteleafe

Snow

Piling in heaps the pure white snow settles,
Waiting for children
To come and play.

The children pour in
And disturb peace
And start making snowballs.

The temperature decreases,
Puddles turn to ice
And icicles are created.

The children make snowmen,
With huge balls of snow,
Made for the next day.

A ray of sun,
In the afternoon,
Beams a signal.

The snow is melting,
The children come out,
A puddle lies on the floor.

Michael Sims (11)
Whyteleafe Primary School, Whyteleafe

Sticky Toffee

You soothe my mouth with a creamy flavour,
I want a supply of you that will last forever,
You are my love, you are my life,
Eat sticky toffee, that is my advice.

You stick, I bite, I chew, you fight,
I bite, I chew, I go bright blue,
You're like a belt holding my teeth together,
You practically last forever.

All I want to say is, I want one of you every day!

Lorna Dawe (10)
Whyteleafe Primary School, Whyteleafe

Falling Snow

Falling snow, falling snow,
Glittering, shining, sparkling, piling,
Icy pond, icy pond,
Where has all the life gone?

Freezing air, freezing air
Stop blowing over the garden chair,
Slippery grass, slippery grass,
Stop tripping passers-by up and fast.

Oh how, oh how,
Oh why, oh why,
Oh what, oh what
Made the weatherman lie?

At three o'clock in the afternoon,
There's a ray of hope, the sun's coming soon.

Falling snow, falling snow,
Glittering, shining, sparkling, piling,
The sun has shone,
The snow has gone.

Shining sun, shining sun,
Welcome laughter,
Welcome fun,
But I can't help missing that cool breeze
Of snow, snow, snow.

Eleanor Williams (10)
Whyteleafe Primary School, Whyteleafe

Evil

Destruction is everywhere
Nothing can stop it
This man has the mind of the Devil
He sleeps in the flaming furnaces of Hell

Evil is this untamed beast

He carries the message that all mankind will fall
He rides at the dead of night
His eyes are as red as fire
He rides on a bloodthirsty stallion
That crushes anything that gets in its path

Run, run as fast as you can because you will fall into the Devil's hand
You will be petrified at the sight of this monstrosity
He is the right hand man of chaos
Shadows are where the domain of this beast is

Many men have never been seen again after they enter this lair
Of such a destructive monster
His main nemesis is the kind and helpful peace
Who will sacrifice himself for our humanity?

This beast is trying to take over the world
He drinks the souls of people
People hide under their covers praying for justice and mercy
You can hear the shrieks of children
Dogs barking
Mothers screaming
Fathers leaping in terror
Try to hold onto your mind and soul
Ha, ha, ha.

James Daly (10)
Whyteleafe Primary School, Whyteleafe